2
10/06

COOL TOOLS

COOL TOOLS

Cooking Utensils from the Japanese Kitchen

Kate Klippensteen

PHOTOGRAPHS BY Yasuo Konishi

STYLING BY Ori Koyama

KODANSHA INTERNATIONAL
Tokyo • New York • London

Distributed in the United States by Kodansha America Inc.,
and in the United Kingdom and continental Europe by Kodansha
Europe Ltd.

Published by Kodansha International, Ltd., 17-14 Otowa 1-chome,
Bunkyo-ku, Tokyo 112-8652, and Kodansha America, Inc.

ISBN-13: 978-4-7700-3016-0
ISBN-10: 4-7700-3016-9

First Edition, 2006
15 14 13 12 11 10 09 08 07 06   10 9 8 7 6 5 4 3 2 1

Library of Congress Catalog-in-Publication Data available.

www.kodansha-intl.com

Contents

PREFACE   7

THE PREPARATION   10

Knives ▪ Mortar and Pestle ▪ Sesame and Gingko Nut Toasters ▪ Copper Grater ▪ Sharkskin Grater ▪ "Devil Grater" ▪ Bonito Plane ▪ Metal Pots ▪ Strainers ▪ Others

THE COOKING   42

Rice Cooker ▪ Steamer ▪ *Donabe* Ceramic Pot ▪ Ceramic Hot-Plates ▪ Porridge Pot ▪ Copper *Oden* Pot ▪ Bronze Tempura Pot ▪ *Oyakodon* and *Tamagoyaki* Pans ▪ Stirrers and Spatulas ▪ Ladles and Skimmers ▪ Metal Grills ▪ Drop Lids ▪ Sauce Brushes ▪ Cooking Chopsticks ▪ Bamboo Colander ▪ Sieve

THE PRESENTATION   74

Graters ▪ Ladles and Scoops ▪ Serving Chopsticks ▪ *Shamoji* Rice Scoops ▪ Rice Tubs ▪ Rice Rolling Mat ▪ Wooden Rice Molds ▪ *Onigiri* Riceball Molds ▪ Sushi Mold

CLEANING UP   96

Brushes ▪ Cleaning Cloth ▪ Odds and Ends ▪ Style

STOCKING YOUR KITCHEN   107

THE RESTAURANTS ▪ THE SHOPS   108

THE ITEMS   109

ACKNOWLEDGEMENTS   111

Preface

Why a book about kitchen tools?

I wanted to chronicle the beauty and uses of the surprising volume of Japanese cooking utensils. Truth be told, I've always been drawn to tools, primitive or refined. I was the kind of kid who enjoyed trips to the hardware store with my father while my siblings fled from anything that vaguely hinted at chores. In the seventies, the hardware stores of northern California still had rough plank floors and a dizzying array of tools, including rows of tipped galvanized buckets full of nails and bolts. I was attracted to it all, drawn to the very shape and material of hardware. Tool handles were still made of wood and broom bristles of straw (no plastic, please)—and they had the classic feel of belonging in grandpa's shed. Later, when I owned a horse, I would spend hours in a tack shop, poring over the choice of another bit or hoof pick that I would spend my allowance on.

But my interest in Japanese cooking tools was a long time coming. I had seen some of them as a child—my mother made tempura regularly and owned a pair of those imposingly long metal-tipped cooking chopsticks. And later in college, while working as a waitress in a Japanese restaurant in San Francisco, I caught glimpses of the impressive knives, such as the *oroshi-bocho*. I remember stopping to stare in awe (it's a staggeringly long blade for cutting enormous fish such as tuna), and the chef would chase me back to work before starting in on the fish. I also remember the chef's wife bustling about the kitchen gingerly carrying a large pot, steam rising from the hot *dashi* stock, with only a grip. I never tried it; it looked dangerous for a novice. But Japanese chef friends today tell me it's still the best way to work a kitchen efficiently. Pot handles, they say, simply get in the way of the action.

It took years of living in Tokyo before I thought about expanding my Japanese cooking repertoire beyond soba or miso soup. I was single, playing and working hard. I was based in one of the world's finest dining cities and I couldn't be bothered to muddle around in the kitchen when every sort of satisfying dining experience—from the most modest to the wildly extravagant—was available at any hour of day or night. And then, it actually became my "job" to dine out, when I started writing regular food columns in the nineties for Japanese editions of magazines such as *Playboy*, *Esquire* and *Marie Claire*. My kitchen was, needless to say, very neglected.

I was doing a story for *Elle Japon* in Kyoto when I first visited Aritsugu—a tiny shop with more than 400 years of history, crammed with beautifully crafted kitchen tools of steel, aluminum, copper and bronze. The woven silver ladles for scooping out tofu from *nabemono* looked like jewels, the Damascus patterns coursing down the steel knife blades like prints, the pounded pots like *objets d'art*. There was nothing in the shop that I didn't want. After long deliberation, I chose a classic tin-covered copper *oroshigane* grater. There was something about the organic shape and the unexpected weight of the piece that demanded my attention. My cooking tool collection had started.

In my estimation, a major appeal of Japanese kitchen utensils is their organic quality, the result of being handmade. Their shapes are often asymmetrical. The use of natural materials also means that the colors of the tools change through use, as they take on a unique patina. The copper *oden-nabe*, for instance, blackens on the outside, and wooden tools actually change in shape over time.

In sushi restaurants, for example, the massive cutting board counter has to be periodically switched end-to-end, as the head chef stands and cuts in the same position, year-in, year-out. Look closely on your next visit. You can see the worn indentation where he works: the soft curvature makes it seem as if the wood has been caressed by an eroding sea.

Shamoji and knife handles mold to the owner's hand through use. In fine restaurants, each cook has his own set of knives for this reason—the knives belong to the user alone, becoming an extension of the body. To use another's knife would be like sticking your feet into someone else's well-worn shoes.

Junichiro Tanizaki, in his classic short essay on Japanese aesthetics, "In Praise of Shadows," condemns the Western bathroom for being too shiny and sterile. The same could be said about Western cooking tools.

Though some people will pay fantastic amounts for premium cookware lines, to me they don't call out to be coveted. Their shape and material are excellent for enduring high-powered washing machines, but they're too sleek and uniform to be lovable. You can have the long-lasting newness of stainless utensils; I'll take a tool that feels "alive," one that speaks of its history in the kitchen.

Are they works of art? I like to believe so, despite the many craftspeople who have insisted that function was foremost in their minds during the creation process. These workmen have little time for the ornamental cook-ware of, say, Alessi or Philippe Starck. Their objectives are tools that are easy to use and easy to repair, and meant to last a lifetime. That's not a boast to be taken lightly. The hammered pot, for example, does become a bit wobbly after long use, and can be returned to the maker to be pounded back into shape. The worn teeth of the oroshigane can be hammered out individually. (I've had two graters of different sizes repaired over the years.) Of course, you pay more for these goods, but you'll find it harder to part with them.

Like Japan's cuisine, the tools in this book are highly refined, designed with the unique needs of specific dishes. I have been cooking Japanese dishes now for eight years, and have yet to use all the tools featured here. But I've begun to understand—and deeply appreciate—the subtle features of the ones I do use. When I cook for friends in Lisbon or San Francisco, I lament that I haven't brought my fish or vegetable knives—oh, how a sharp knife alone would make a difference! And I can assure you that wasabi

grated on a sharkskin grater does taste different from the same root grated on copper—the sweetness is accentuated.

When I first arrived in Tokyo, the bubble economy was raging and Japanese were obsessed with buying the best from the West. Traditional cooking tools were being replaced with stainless Henckel knives, Le Creuset pots and so on. Many housewives embraced plastic, too, believing it was modern and hygienic. But I'm happy to report that this thinking was relatively short-lived (though still embraced by some). Today, there is a keen interest in traditional cooking tools and materials.

My neighbor drives to Tsukiji, the wholesale fish market, to buy dried whole bonito to shave on a bonito plane once used by her mother. Her husband delights in telling me that their ten-year-old son can taste the difference between freshly shaved and store packaged. I know an editor who's an excellent cook. Her kitchen is far from professional, but each tool she has is finely handcrafted. And scores of friends have given up on the electric rice cooker, using *donabe* earthenware or the traditional cast iron *okama*.

Meanwhile, bamboo strainers, which Sacheverell Sitwell described in his 1959 travel essay on Japan, "The Bridge of the Brocade Sash," as "the most attractive objects," are back in fashion. Today, if you rummage around the kitchen on a visit to an average home you'll find pasta cooking pots, enamel pots and pressure cookers. But among them you'll also find the true showstoppers—relatives of the beautiful handcrafted Japanese tools on the following pages.

As the worldwide familiarity with Japanese cuisine increases and the palates of so many diners become even more sophisticated, I hope people will stop to contemplate and enjoy the history and culture, the art and function of these wonderful tools.

The Preparation

Is Japanese cuisine intimidating to make? Not really. Its preparation, or *shikomi*, however, can be tricky, since a typical repast involves a number of dishes called *okazu*, which precede the finale of rice and soup. The petite plates on which these dishes are served can easily add up to two dozen (making an equally laborious chore for the dishwasher).

So yes, the preparation is intensive, and it starts at the shops to procure the best that the season offers—squid in summer, rape blossom in spring, bonito in the fall. . . . Back in the kitchen, preparation requires concentration and a flurry of multi-tasking. There is the early washing of the rice so it has to time to dry before steaming, and the tossing of *konbu* seaweed into a pot to start the soup stock. While waiting for water to boil for spinach, a *yamaimo* mountain potato will be grated into a sticky froth. Knives flash as fish are gutted, eggs whisked and vegetables washed and strained. Then the konbu is removed from the stock to be replaced by a handful of fresh shavings of bonito flakes. A quick turn to skim the foam from items on the boil, and—with the switching on of the rice cooker—preparation is complete.

A handcrafted Japanese knife can be awe-inspiring. Stately, spiritual and stunningly beautiful with its fine edge, damascus patterns or *kita-eji hada* (literally "hammered metal skin") and buffalo horn bolster, it demands to be handled with care and treasured for years.

The lineage of these powerful blades can be traced through the tradition of swordsmiths. These highly skilled artisans began fashioning knives for the aristocracy when nationwide peace in the Edo Period slowed the demand for swords. The final blow for sword makers came when the Meiji government banned sword bearing altogether, and many artisans shifted their complete attention to knives.

Chefs worldwide are now the beneficiaries of those historic government policies; the **yanagi-ba** (top) and **deba-bocho** were both made using sword-crafting techniques.

The sturdy **deba-bocho** is used to gut and fillet fish and cut up poultry. The part of the blade nearest the handle, not the tip, is used to cut through bones; the blade is thick enough to take quite a beating, so the cook need not worry about chipping. This type of knife is also used to pound shrimp into a paste and to chop raw fish, including bonito and horse mackerel, for serving in a style called *tataki* (meaning "to chop").

To prepare tataki, the fish is gutted and the head removed. The body is separated in three places from the tail (called *sanmai-oroshi*). The bones and skin are removed and the fish is chopped and minced with scallions and grated ginger. In areas of the Boso Peninsula, east of Tokyo, the minced fish is sometimes mixed with miso into a patty, then grilled like a hamburger to create a wonderfully aromatic dish called *sangayaki*.

The deba-bocho comes in small, medium and large sizes. The blade length starts at three inches for small fish like sardines and increases to an impressive twelve inches or more for tuna and other big fish. The knife shown here is sold under the Danjuro line at Kiya, a purveyor of kitchen tools for more than 200 years. The line is named for the famous Kabuki actor, Ichikawa Danjuro, after Kiya's founder won the right to use the illustrious name in the Meiji Period. The name is a revered title and is handed down—the current Ichikawa Danjuro XII is said to use these knives.

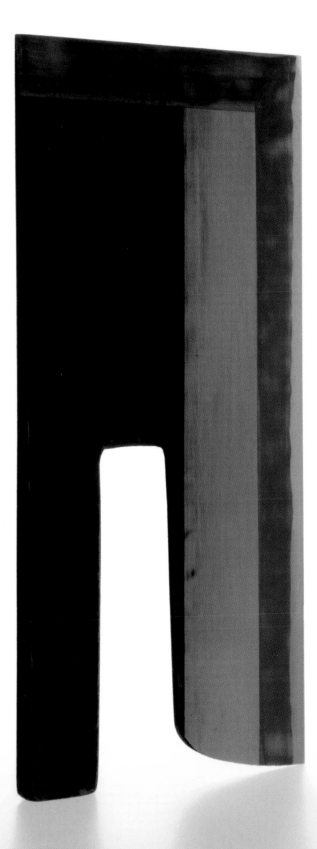

There is something vaguely Brancusian about this **soba-bocho**, or **menkiri-bocho**—which literally means "noodle cutting knife." The simple, hefty, axe-like blade will cut evenly through fifteen to twenty layers of dough. It's not by accident that some soba shops have their kneading and cutting stations facing the window. Passersby will stop and gaze at a soba maker skillfully pushing the massive knife through the stacked layers of buckwheat dough, and suddenly decide that a dish of noodles is just the thing for lunch.

Until the spread of post-war prosperity, buckwheat soba and dumplings were widely served as a nutritious substitute to rice when rice crops were poor. The soba dish was what is known now as *inaka* ("country") soba, a thick noodle of ninety to one hundred percent soba flour. Many friends over forty have shared their recollections of a mother or grandmother deftly handling the soba-bocho. But today, what was once prosaic fare has been elevated to haute cuisine. Soba devotees will spend significant time and money in a famous soba shop, where the idea is to linger over sake and appetizers in a build-up to the finale of fine *seiro* noodles.

The popularity of soba has sparked a boom in soba parties, usually presided over by the man of the house—resulting in dozens of soba cookbooks targeting male soba-master aspirants.

The *yanagi-ba*, the long, willowy *sashimi* knife (and this is not just a turn of phrase—*yanagi* means "willow," and *ba* means "blade") has a cult-like following around the world. In Japan, the knife is just another everyday tool, serving a specific function; most kitchens have one. At home, the yanagi-ba will be of reasonably high quality, partly processed by machine, partly by hand, and cost around one hundred dollars. These versions have blades that are relatively short, around eight inches, which makes them easier and safer to manipulate. But the pros also use much longer blades. The longest blade shown here in the center is thirteen inches. The sashimi knife with the squared head is called a *tako-biki* (octopus knife), and was developed in the Kanto area around Tokyo. It was crafted by arguably Japan's finest knife maker, Tokifusa Iizuka who, with his two sons, makes his knives entirely by hand, from forging to grinding to polishing. In fact, it takes an entire day to make just one knife. This one, inscribed with Iizuka's trade name, Shigefusa, costs more than eight hundred dollars.

Most chefs stick to the conventional, Kansai (Osaka)-style yanagi-ba with the pointed end. The reason is that even small fish, such as sardines or shad, can be cleaned and cut without switching knives. Chefs committed to the tako-biki have to drop it in favor of a smaller *deba-bocho* knife to take care of smaller fish.

Vegetables matter. A Japanese meal includes a smattering of fish, soy and meat protein, but almost all dishes feature vegetables. It's not surprising then that two knives are used when working with vegetables: the *nakiri-bocho* (on the opposite page) and the *usuba-bocho*. These knives are different from others in that their blades are thin and straight, for cutting vegetables clean through, with almost no pressure needed.

The nakiri-bocho is the standard vegetable knife and most kitchens have one. (Na-kiri means literally "to cut vegetables.") It is used to slice small eggplant, to split cabbage heads, dice potatoes and carrots, chop onions and many other tasks. The tip of the back edge is usually squared like this one, though the Kansai-style knives are rounded on the back tip as well as the front. The cutting edge is also angled from both sides, called *ryoba*, making it easier to cut straight slices.

The usuba-bocho is often used by professionals, and differs from the nakiri in that it is sharpened from one side, in a style called *kataba*. Some kataba blades have a slight depression on the flat side, which gives an even better cut. It allows the cook to do the intricate shaping of vegetables into maple leaves or cherry blossoms and for the paper-thin slices of Chinese radish and carrot that one sees in fine restaurants.

Whether it is a nakiri or usuba, there is something soothingly rhythmic about a chef chopping vegetables rapid-fire down the cutting board.

In fine Japanese restaurants, chefs meticulously maintain their personal knife sets, which usually consist of around thirteen blades. In the process of creating a full-course meal, they will use only knives specific to the task—*sashimi* and vegetable knives, beef knives, boning knives, big- and small-fish knives, conger eel knives and more. But how many knives must amateur chefs own to navigate their way through a Japanese menu? The people at Aritsugu of Kyoto, who have made knives for more than four hundred years, say that this quintet—"The Five Basic Knives Every Household Should Stock"—is all one needs.

From left, here's the one Western import, the petty knife, which is fairly popular for cutting and peeling vegetables and fruit. Many cooks feel that the Japanese version's thin, razor sharp blade distinguishes it from its European counterpart.

The *yanagi-ba*, or sashimi knife, is designed to cut cleanly through fish in one go, from tip to grip, and is essential for clean, even sashimi slices.

The heavy *deba-bocho* is used to fillet fish. It is also used for cutting through hard bones, like those in fish heads, and for cleaving whole birds, turtles and lobsters. The relatively thick blade prevents chipping.

The *santoku-bocho* is the universal knife. It is unusual for a Japanese knife in that its blade is symmetrically pitched on both sides. It is suitable for cutting vegetables—which can make up eighty percent of a Japanese meal—fish and meat. In other words: the perfect knife. Its only fault is that it can chip easily.

The *usuba-bocho* is a vegetable knife. It has a fine, straight blade suitable for cutting all the way down to the cutting board without a horizontal pull or push. The usuba is often used for refined work, such as the seemingly impossible intricate peeling of vegetables and fruit.

"**I** love my *suribachi*. I hold it close to me every morning. . . .

"But seriously, a chef must have affection for his mortar. For me, grinding the sesame for *goma-dofu* is the most critical element of *shojin* cuisine, the vegetarian, Zen-temple cooking I serve in my restaurant. The two Chinese characters for shojin could be translated as 'advancement of the spirit,' a reference to our striving, through Buddhist training, to attain purity of body and spirit. In this respect, grinding sesame is not just my ritual of daily food preparation, but a part of Zen.

There are three important points in shojin cuisine: sincerity, cleanliness and gratitude. Every morning, I start my day by dousing myself with cold water. I then give my restaurant a thorough cleaning. And every single morning, following that, I make sesame tofu—with sincerity as well as gratitude, to the forces of nature that provided the seeds.

I grind by moving the pestle in a circular fashion, for thirty minutes to an hour. The grinding is rigorous—if you're not used to it you will really feel it in your chest and shoulders. I personally grind the sesame to the left, and create an *uzu* or vortex; in this way, I build energy and focus it. The circle is the universe, and I eventually become one with the mortar and pestle and seed. It is no coincidence that sitting Zen-style and drawing the universe is a fundamental part of a monk's training.

Toshio Tanahashi

Chef
Gesshinkyo

Mix, grind or mash . . . who needs a cumbersome food processor? In a Japanese kitchen, the elegant *suribachi* mortar works just fine.

While the outside of the glazed pottery mortar is smooth, the inside is combed into fine, jagged grooves, perfect for transforming ingredients into pastes and powders. The *kogi* pestle is made of wood, which is not only gentle on the suribachi, but—since every pestle leaves a little of itself on the grooves of the mortar—is also kind to the food. Although many types of wood can be used, this kogi, for example, is made from the pepper tree, which adds a hint of fragrance to the food being processed.

The easiest way to use the mortars, which range up to thirty centimeters in diameter, is to place them on the floor on a non-slip surface, such as a damp cloth, and grind with the pestle from a kneeling position.

The pestle may be used to grind sesame seeds for pale, quivering *goma-dofu*, which despite its name contains no soy (it is almost entirely made of sesame with a bit of arrowroot flour). Or, to mash broad beans for a chilled summer soup, or small red *azuki* beans for sweets, or to grind fish paste for dumplings.

More evocative than a whirring blender, the muted thumping of the wooden kogi against the sides of the ceramic vessel whets the appetite.

The *suribachi*, which has been used in cooking since the Edo Period, should be replaced from time to time as the grooves are dulled through use (traditionally the grooves in the ceramic clay were made using pine needles). A chef's mortar, used daily, might need replacing after eight to ten years. In most homes, however, the vessel functions perfectly for a generation.

The two *goma-iri* (top and bottom) are used for toasting sesame seeds (goma), widely used in cooking and as a garnish. Sesame is sprinkled on a bowl of rice or soba noodles, or on cooked vegetables. Larger amounts are toasted before being ground into paste for mixing with arrowroot flour to make goma-dofu, or for making a delicate sesame dressing. The metal-screened goma-iri and *ginnan-iri* (center)—which is similarly used for toasting gingko nuts—are held over an open flame at a distance that prevents burning, before being flipped over the mortar to discharge their contents. The ceramic goma-iri can be placed directly over a flame for more evenly distributed heat; the open handle also acts as a funnel for pouring the roasted sesame into a grinder.

The metal versions of these tools are relatively new, dating to the Meiji Period; the ceramic goma-iri probably came into use in the Edo Period.

Oroshigane are used to grate *daikon* radish and mountain potato, as well as ginger and wasabi. This copper oroshigane is the standard shape, though they are made in many sizes.

Copper is the most suitable material for the oroshigane—ensuring that the teeth will be neither too hard nor soft. For copper graters like this one, a thin copper sheet is first pounded with a spring hammer to strengthen the metal before being cut by hand into the classic shape. After being plated in tin, the teeth are then cut and raised tooth by tooth—a painstaking job still done by hand. (Any handmade grater with worn teeth can be refurbished.)

This oroshigane is used almost exclusively to grate wasabi, the pungent yet sweet "horseradish" that complements sushi and other dishes. It consists simply of a piece of shark-skin nailed to a natural wood board. Sharkskin has been used in Japan for centuries, most notably in sword grips, and here its rough texture—similar to the coarsest sandpaper—makes for a finer grating surface than metal graters provide. Many chefs believe that metal is too harsh for grating was-abi; others say the extra pressure needed to grate on shark-skin does a better job of releasing wasabi's volatile flavor.

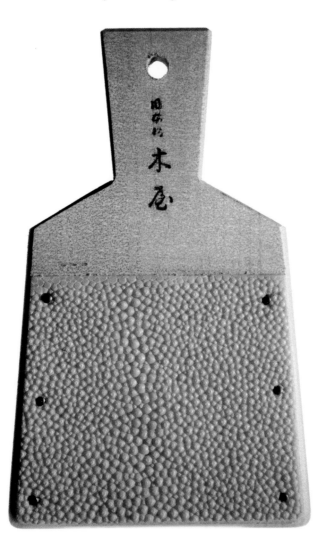

This curious-looking bamboo implement is used for grating *daikon* radish—so coarsely that the resulting mash provides a robust texture for various recipes.

Called an **oni oroshi**, or "devil grater," the utensil takes its name from a dish popular in Tochigi and Ibaraki prefectures. Beans are used in the Setsubun rite of early February, in which evil spirits are chased from homes by inhabitants throwing roasted beans and shouting, "Out with the devil!" According to the tale, some resourceful cook gathered the leftover beans, crushed and formed them into balls and made a stew, adding rough chunks of daikon and carrots to the *dashi* stock. The grater was created for this—inelegant, perhaps, but easy on the digestion—dish.

Many cooks will argue that soup stock—*dashi*—is the most critical element of Japanese cooking, and will guard their recipes fiercely. Dashi can be concocted from small dried sardines or *konbu* (seaweed) alone, or from stronger ingredients such as shrimp, clams or *shiitake* mushrooms. The standard dashi, however, involves *konbu* followed by *katsuo* bonito flakes, which in Japan can be bought packaged, even from convenience stores. Until about forty years ago, however, most kitchens were equipped with their own **katsuo kezuriki** (bonito plane).

This device is used to shave flakes from whole bonito which, when dried, becomes as hard as wood. This requires practice to create feathery sheets instead of powdery flecks. (The shavings fall into the drawer below, which is opened with the elegant handle.) With the resurgent trend for slow food, many cooks have pulled out their parents' katsuo plane from cupboards and store rooms to return the flavor and fragrance to their kitchens.

These shimmering, easy-to-stack *kuminabe* are both handsome and pleasant to the touch. Yet practicality, not aesthetics, was on the minds of their original designers. When Western metal kitchenware was introduced in the Meiji Period, savvy Japanese cooks remodeled it for their own purposes.

The overriding design principle is that the pots are easy to use and maintain. They are made of aluminum, which is soft but easily strengthened by repeated pounding. The result is lightweight, non-sparking and heat conductive. The pounding also has a secondary benefit, as the resultant dimples prevent sticking and burning. Finally, though easily dented through heavy use, the vessels can readily be repaired, ensuring a lifetime of use.

Kuminabe were designed to fit the stoves in Japanese kitchens, which—in both homes and restaurants—tend to be tiny by Western standards. Handles are done away with, and the vessels are moved over the flame with a *yattoko*, or pliers-like grip. And of course, the lack of handles and easy-stacking mean they require a minimum of shelf space. Ranging in diameter from around six to eleven inches, the pots also serve as measuring cups.

This is the standard *yukihira-nabe*, with high-angled handle, which is found in most homes—though cooks with particularly cramped kitchens might remove the handle and simply use the protruding socket as a grip.

This vessel is handmade in the same way as the stacking pots: two sheets of aluminum are welded together—one for the bottom and the other for the sides. Using only one sheet would mean the aluminum would have to be stretched, and the thickness of the metal would become uneven—affecting the heat dispersion.

Songwriter and singer, 23-years-old
Single household
DIAMETER: 6¼"

Kitchen helper and mother, 40-something
Four-person household
D: 7⅞"

Housewife, 48
Three-person household
D: 7¼"

Japanese language instructor and mother, 52
Five-person household
D: 8½"

Cook, 45-ish
Four-person household
D: 10½"

Bank employee and mother, 40-something
Five-person household
D: 5⅛"

Japanese strainers, or *zaru*, are made from either metal and bamboo, with the former debuting in kitchens of the wealthy during the Meiji Period. However, while metal strainers tend to be of a standard design, the traditional bamboo zaru come in infinite shapes, sizes and patterns of weave.

It is the variety of bamboo that ranks it over stainless steel or enamel in most people's estimate. Like bamboo, zaru have many uses. They can hold a dish of cold soba noodles, for example, or vegetables and fruit being sold at a roadside stand. And in the summer time, fine stores and inns might even wrap gift items in elaborate zaru.

Some shapes denote a specific function, such as that of the *komeagezaru* (at top left), which is used to rinse and strain rice. Notice the lip for pouring off water. The zaru with the short handle is called a strainer-ladle. The smallest strainer is for tea, and the one with the loosest weave might be used to lay out fruit to dry, such as persimmons in the fall.

The Japanese have used bamboo baskets for centuries, with some being unearthed in Jomon-period ruins from as far back as 300 B.C. Millennia later, bamboo artistry remains a hands-on process, and there is something both refreshingly contemporary and ancient in the material's supple luster.

It is often said that bamboo work is a craft that takes full advantage of the natural shape of bamboo, as well as its pliancy. The strainer-ladle with handle on this page perhaps best illustrates this. One piece of bamboo has been split, stripped at the top and shaped to form the frame. (This is the same technique used in making the skeleton for Japanese fans.) Like its smaller brother on the previous page, this strainer is extremely convenient for scooping foods—like noodles, *edamame* soybeans, dumplings, seaweed, etc.—from boiling water. If the cook is making a batch of dumplings, for example, the same boiling water can be used again and again.

The elegant **sobazaru** basket, opposite, is used to serve soba. It sits on a built-in base and has dimples to create corners. Years of experience and much careful work went into both achieving stability and creating an aesthetic balance between the base and upper basket. Most baskets for serving soba are round, and only a handful of weavers has the skill to make such an elaborate one. The basketmaker obviously believed this zaru should be capable not only of holding soba, but also sweets. Or, more grandly, perhaps, a portion of fragrant tempura.

Examine the cupboards of a Japanese chef and you will doubtless find some of these tools. At left are several *yasai nukigata*, the razor-sharp, stainless-steel vegetable cutters used to punch shapes of maple leaves or cherry blossoms. Cut from raw carrots or *daikon* radish, they adorn New Year's recipes and clear broth soups.

Next are three of the countless utensils used in preparing sea-creatures: the fish deboner **honenuki**; the oyster knife, or **kaki-nuki**; and the fish-scaler—**urokotori**. The latter is indispensable, as most markets sell fish whole, and though fishmongers will scale and gut fish on request, many cooks perform the task themselves. The traditional scaler is better than a knife, since it eliminates the risk of cutting the skin—the fish's or your own.

The bamboo scraper, or **sukureipa**, is for the highly specific chore of cleaning the fine teeth of graters, which become entangled with the fibers of ingredients such as ginger.

Finally, no kitchen is complete without bundles of **kushi**, or skewers. These are used to pierce and hold food for grilling and frying—*yakitori* chicken, *kushiyaki* morsels, small croquettes and the many mashed fish- and vegetable-based tidbits in *oden* stew. Ranging in size from six to fourteen inches, kushi are made of steel, wood or bamboo. Even something as simple as bamboo skewers come in some very unique designs, shaped for easy gripping, for example, or with twisted ends.

The Cooking

The cooking itself, or *chori*, takes place at a little less frenetic tempo than the preparation. Many food items are slowly grilled or simmered. Nevertheless, there are multiple pots on the stove and several items on grills going simultaneously, making the timing extremely vital. Value is placed not only on the raw ingredients, but also on the "freshly cooked" impact of the food when it hits the palate.

So the cook, who is working with several—say ten—dishes, will start and stagger cooking to ensure the food arrives at the table at the correct time and temperature. Vegetable dishes served chilled or at room temperature will be started early, as well as foods requiring long simmering. Stir-frys are left until the last minute, and so, too, the miso soup. Skilled chefs will have the broth of the classic soup ready and waiting—the miso bean paste is stirred in just prior to serving to ensure that all-important freshness.

Who would have thought that this *okama*, a commanding, cast-iron vessel crowned with a heavy cypress lid, was the precursor to the banal-looking electric rice-cooker?

The life-giving grain has long been a staple of the islands that now make up Japan. Ceramic rice-cookers, which sat on openings in *kamado*, or platform-like clay stoves, date back to at least the Kofun Period (310–710), and were common until their replacement by the cast-iron okama in the Edo Period. These were superseded by electric models in the decades following World War II.

The vessel featured here is made of *nanbu tekki* cast ironware from Iwate Prefecture—long famed for its sturdy and beautiful ironwork. Cast-iron is the preferred material for boiling water or making rice because it doesn't taint the flavor of the water. (Not surprisingly, the Iwate region also contributes teapots and other vessels for the tea ceremony.) The lid of the okama is substantial, since the vessel must function somewhat like a pressure cooker.

Traditionally, okama were used over an open hearth, or set into a purpose-built depression on the top of wood-burning stoves. Though not many kitchens are equipped with either feature these days, increasing numbers of home chefs are using okama in their modern kitchens—gamely putting them directly on conventional gas stoves—in their quest for the perfect bowl of rice. Rice lovers insist that the okama is superior to the electric cooker for many reasons, mainly the higher heat intensity the iron pot delivers. The heat from electric cookers is weak, and so rice, or any other food, takes longer to cook—at the expense of flavor. And iron holds the heat longer than the aluminum inserts of electric cookers, which is of extreme importance as the grain is transformed into its ideal, fluffy result. (Japanese say *okome ga tatsu* or the "rice stands up.")

The okama is very simple to use. Wash and dry the rice, as when using a rice cooker, and use the same water-to-rice ratio. Start on a low flame and turn it up when steam appears. Then wait for the scent of slight burning, which adds a lovely flavor to the rice. Turn off the heat and let the rice steam for about ten minutes. A chef friend who insists on using an okama says the result is superior in every way: texture, moisture balance and taste—and it takes half the time of a machine.

Waseiro, or Japanese steamers, are used for much more than preparing vegetables. These beautiful, handmade cypress utensils are often employed in the home in place of microwaves—to steam and reheat leftovers, from rice to stir-fry dishes. (Simply steam hardened rice in a cloth draped in the basket and the rice will be returned to its moist and light, just-cooked state.)

Chinese buns and *gyoza* dumplings are commonly steamed in this vessel, as are yams and even fillets of eel. The steamer is also used to make dishes such as *sekihan*—the rice steamed pink with azuki beans and served on auspicious occasions such as Girl's Day—or *chawanmushi*, the savory egg custard of chicken and gingko nuts that warms up wintry days.

The rather hefty lid acts to keep the steam in, and the steamer's height prevents burns on the cook's hands. The body is made of cypress, which is heat resistant and therefore durable. The intricate closure is made of strong cherry tree bark, and the seat, or *sunoko*, is made of strips of bamboo and supported by two braces of *sawara*, a type of cypress.

The *donabe*, a ceramic pot, is one of Japan's oldest cooking utensils, with archaeologists dating its use to over 10,000 years ago. What the ancients stewed up, however, is debated. Today, it is undoubtedly *nabemono*, the one-pot dish of vegetables with accompanying ingredients ranging from tofu to cod, salmon, oysters or chicken, all simmered in a rich broth.

The enjoyment of nabemono was first documented 200 years ago. It has been popular ever since—as the perfect antidote to bitter winter days. What a pleasure it is, to snuggle in with family or friends around a low table where the communal donabe simmers over a gas burner. Ingredients are added from platters; then each diner removes portions into a personal dipping sauce, usually *ponzu* (a mixture of soy sauce, citrus juice, vinegar and soup stock). By the time the piles of food on the platters have dwindled, the broth is wonderfully rich—and not to be wasted: depending on the diners' predilection, udon noodles or rice will now be added to absorb the broth, making for a satisfying conclusion to the meal.

This donabe was fired at the Iga kilns in Mie Prefecture, central Japan, which have produced cooking vessels since the sixteenth century. It has a black glaze called *kuro raku*, which is somewhat unusual for Iga pottery (the makers of which tend to work with the natural color of the clay). The porous nature of Iga clay is excellent for donabe, since it can withstand high flames, and distributes and holds heat efficiently. Those in the know remember to pour a little water into the pots before heating, to prevent the ceramic from cracking.

These two **toban**, or ceramic hotplates, at left are, like the donabe on the previous page, *kuro raku* (black glaze) from Iga. More common in Kansai than other areas of the country, toban are used in the same way as the more popular *teppan* (on which *teppanyaki* is made). A platter of raw, thinly sliced beef or pork and assorted vegetables is brought to the table and diners grill what they desire, eating the morsels hot off the toban. Since presentation is ever-important in Japanese cuisine, many gourmets prefer the sleek ceramic platters to an electric metal grill.

The **yukihira-donabe** on this page most closely resembles Japan's early cooking vessels. But today the pudgy clay pots are used primarily for making *okayu* or *ojiya*, the names for savory rice porridge. Leftover rice and soup often form the base of okayu; the chef then adds vegetables such as leeks and cabbage (and sometimes chicken), topping the lot with bonito flakes. One friend from America, new to Japan, will never forget dropping by her favorite *izakaya* pub one day when she was feeling weary. The master said, "Forget the menu," and putting a yukihira-donabe on the stove, whipped her up an okayu of *konbu* seaweed stock, rice and whisked egg. Her spirits lifted right away. She had discovered the Japanese cure-all: for ailments including upset stomachs, chills and fever—and sometimes just the blues.

This beautiful copper pot, lined in tin, is an **oden nabe** for boiling oden, a stew that traces its beginnings to the Heian Period. A very popular winter dish, oden includes assorted fish cakes—made of white fish or shrimp—*daikon*, egg, *konbu* ties, *konnyaku* devil's tongue, fried *tofu* and burdock root, all bobbing in a soy-rich *dashi* broth. (In the Kansai region, beef is sometimes added.) On a cold winter night, the rich scent rising from an oden street stall is irresistible to passersby. Sitting around the raised rectangular bubbling pot, customers point to the foods they care to sample. The master ladles them into bowls with a dash of broth and a dab of spicy Japanese mustard.

Home-cooks also prepare oden, but usually buy ready-made ingredients at the supermarket. In addition to the elegant copper nabe, which though expensive is best for dispersing heat, aluminum and stainless-steel oden nabe are also available. Many cooks prefer to use an oden nabe that can be placed at the table—its heat source a propane-can-powered, camping-style stove. Proof of oden's popularity are the oden nabe complete with boiling bits of octopus that adjoin the cash register at Japanese convenience stores during winter. My advice? This type of oden is best avoided. Look for a street stall instead.

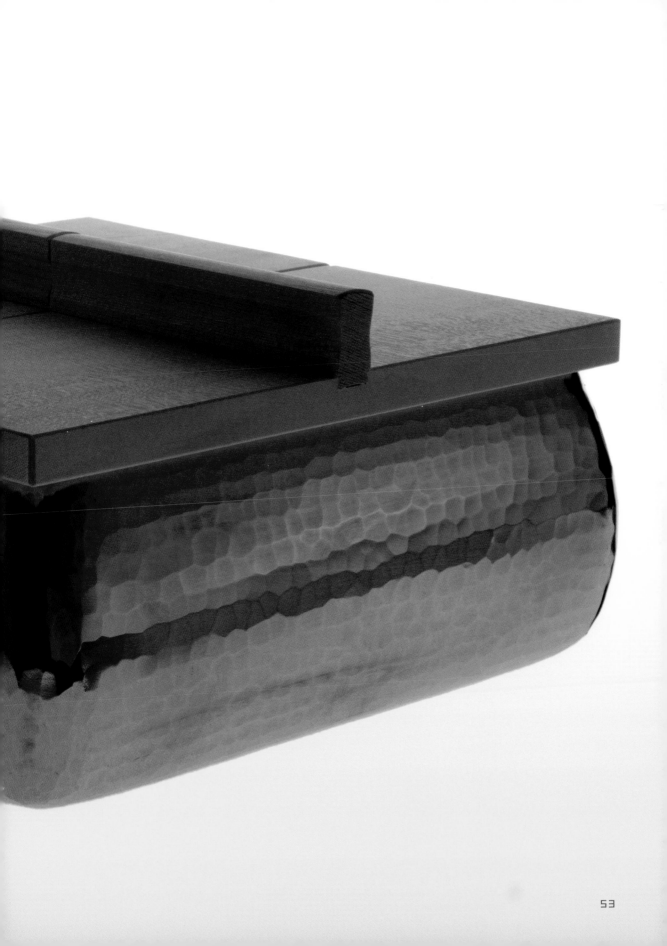

This exquisite bronze *tempura nabe* is not for every household—in fact, its price tag of roughly six hundred dollars makes it a prohibitive purchase for all but the most elegant restaurant. But the rich luster of bronze is peerless when it comes to pleasing the eye. And it's even better than copper, also used as tempura-nabe material, because of its excellent capacity to maintain even temperatures, essential to tasty tempura.

Portuguese merchants are thought to have introduced tempura some four hundred years ago, when they first began trading with Japan. The dish didn't take off, however, until the late Edo Period, when Tokyo street vendors started selling locally caught fish, lightly battered and deep fried.

Today, tempura is a specialized cuisine, like sushi, that most Japanese leave to the professionals to make in restaurants. But once in a while, a cook will get the itch to make tempura at home—in spite of the mess involved—so many kitchens are equipped with an aluminum version of this pot.

There are a number of tricks to getting tempura right: slice the ingredients very thinly so that they fry quickly (about two minutes for vegetables). Fry in small batches to maintain the oil temperature (about 350 degrees F). And be sure to use a deep walled pot, something as close as possible to the shape of this tempura nabe.

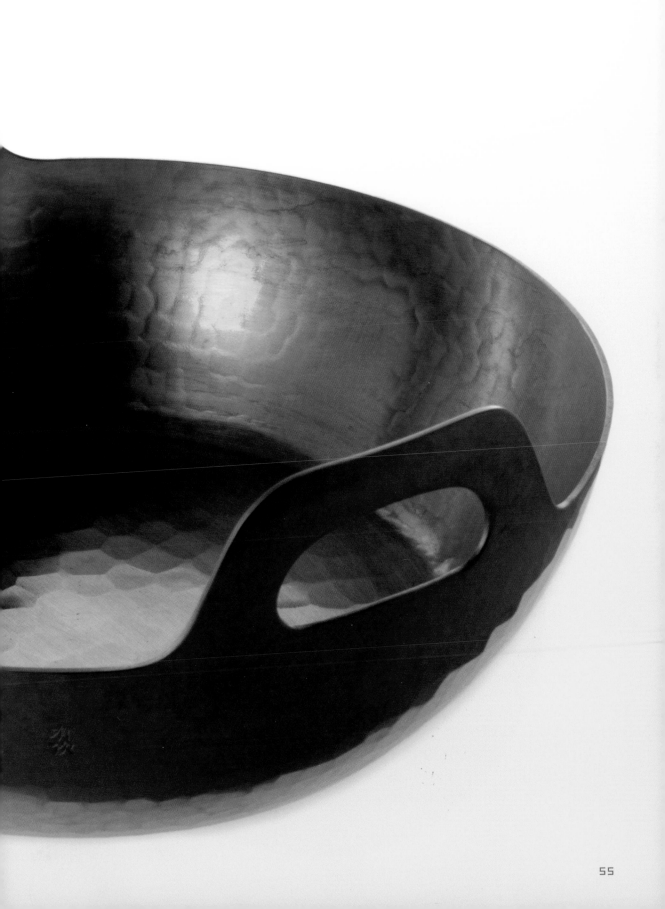

This **oyakonabe** is used primarily in making *oyakodonburi*, which explains its name. *Oya-ko* means "parent and child," reflecting the use of chicken and egg in the dish. Making *oyakodon* is very simple and quick—a fine example of Japanese comfort food. Heat a mixture of dashi, a little soy sauce, water and mirin in the skillet then cook onion slices for two to three minutes. Add bite-size pieces of chicken and scallions, cut lengthwise to an inch or two. When the chicken is cooked through, pour a beaten egg over the mixture and simmer until it reaches a semi-solid state. Slide the combination from the skillet onto a steaming bowl of rice. Oyakodon meals are cooked one at a time; the chef holds the skillet over the low flame for a few minutes, pours the creation onto the rice and gets right to work on the next one. The long, upright handle is useful for this dexterous work.

Ever wonder how sushi shops roll such perfect *mille-feuille* omelets? Though the box-like **tamagoyaki nabe** makes light work of achieving the shape, creating those beautiful layers is a painstaking craft. The cook lightly covers the tin-lined bottom of the copper pan with oil then pours in a thin layer of eggs mixed with *dashi*, soy sauce and brown sugar. After a moment of cooking, the chef, wielding long, kitchen chopsticks, rolls the egg to the head of the *nabe*. Another layer is added and the cook deftly uses one hand on the handle, the other on the chopsticks to wrap the previously rolled first layer in the second. And so it goes, taking great care to avoid sticking—especially tricky due to the sugar—until the nabe is full. The omelet simply slips out of the tray to be carefully sliced and served.

"People today have forgotten that Japanese dishes were traditionally prepared according to the principle of *in-yo* (or yin and yang), the metaphysical concept of the complementary and opposing forces found in all matter. Take the *kataba* blade, for example, which is sharpened on one side. It makes for a beautiful cut of sashimi, but also reflects perfectly the principle in food preparation. You slice into the fish, turn it over and place the rectangular slices on a round plate . . . there is yin and yang at work here, too. You should never present square or rectangular yin food on square or rectangular and deep yin plates—or round or flat yang foods on yang plates. You should also never serve only yin food. You must have a balance.

This balance was a rule for traditional Japanese cuisine, and the chef could play within the rule's boundaries, but was always conscious of it. With a traditional Japanese meal, you should be able to eat and never feel full. Because of the balance and all the vegetables, digestion should only take twenty to forty minutes, leaving the diner feeling invigorated instead of lethargic. A meal with meat, on the other hand, means four hours of digestive work for your stomach.

Too often, in homes and in restaurants, cooking and eating have fallen out of balance. In restaurants, there is too much performance. Chefs want to make a splash by using only extravagant materials. But there should be a build up to something extravagant. If each course is a star and each course itself rich—say, foie gras topped with caviar—it is obvious that the balance has been forgotten. And I can assure you that you won't feel good after the meal. Through my restaurant, books and classes, I'm trying to bring back the balance in eating, which really translates into 'living.'"

Hiromitsu Nozaki

Chef
Waketokuyama

The *hera* or spatula is a relative newcomer to the Japanese kitchen, although various types of hera have been in use for hundreds of years—in carpentry, painting and lacquering.

Hera are generally made of the durable but lightweight wood *chisha*—a type of persimmon tree native to Japan. Beech and cypress are also used. Of the hera featured here, the two that most resemble Western spatulas are made of beech, and are used when cooking with large or deep pots. The three hera of chisha look alike, but perform different functions. The most slender is used in stir-frying, the medium-sized hera is used to push ingredients through a sieve and the largest is used to flip ingredients when frying. Some cooks use small hera in place of brushes to dress a food item with sauce. This is possible, since chisha wood is very pliant. For the same reason, chefs prefer using hera over regular spatulas when pushing miso, chestnut or sweet potato through sieves. The springiness of the wood speeds the straining process.

Japanese ladles and skimmers, called *otama* and *shakushi*, are commonly made of aluminum or wood; bronze examples are rarer and more highly prized. Since these tools are largely hand pounded or carved, they have slightly asymmetrical, one-of-a-kind shapes.

Of course, wood was the material used in ancient times, and today these wooden utensils have been making a comeback as servers—valued now for their "organic" appeal—and used when presenting hearty stews and *nabemono* at the table. The handsome brass shakushi shown here has a wooden handle about twenty inches long, and is found almost exclusively in temples and fine restaurants, although households used to stock them in the days when marriages and funerals were held in the home, and large quantities of food were prepared in big pots.

Undoubtedly, aluminum ladles—which are lightweight and easy to care for—are the most common scoops found in homes today. The bowls of the two aluminum ladles shown here are of different depths, but even so are quite shallow by Western standards. There are at least two reasons for this: Japanese cuisine is served in smaller portions, and, with all the boiling and simmering that goes on for one meal, skimming is an equally important function—one that calls for a flatter bowl. Also, small amounts of soup stock are often ladled into different containers for other purposes, say to add to ground sesame and miso to make a *goma-ae* sauce for vegetables.

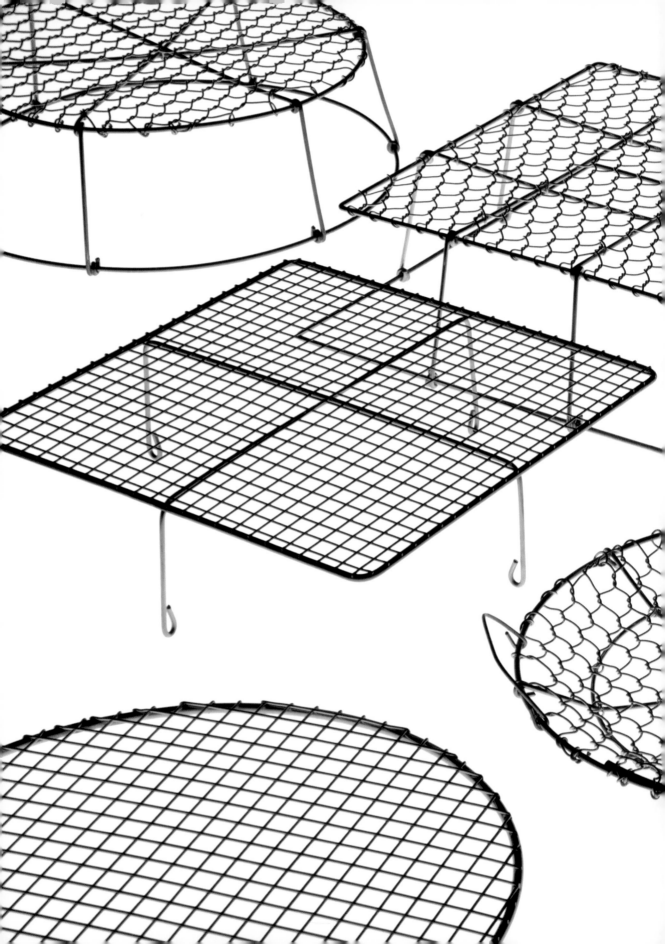

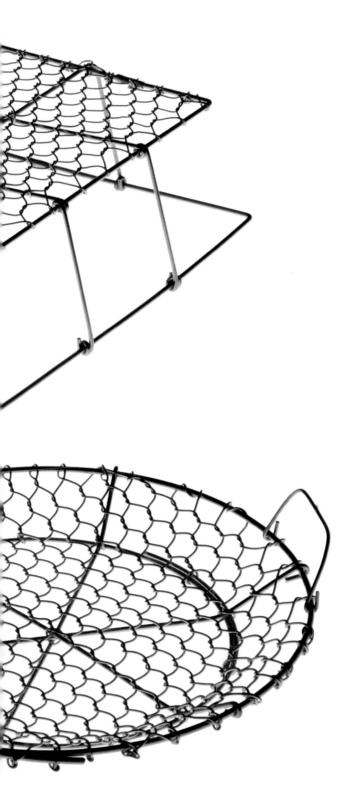

Grilling is a frequent practice in the Japanese kitchen, and though most modern homes have built-in grills in their stove ranges, this may have less to do with convenience than population density. As anyone who has broiled Japanese fish favorites like sardines or horse mackerel directly on the stove can attest, the strong smell lingers—and even overwhelms neighboring homes.

Still, most cooks own a variety of these mesh *yakiami* for grilling vegetables and fish. Yaki-ami are also used throughout the winter—and especially at New Year's—to toast little round or rectangular shaped *mochi* rice cakes, trans-forming the hard blocks into crispy, chewy snacks. Concerned about leftover rice? Many cooks will make rice balls and grill them slowly over a flame, turning them from time to time and eventually glazing them with soy sauce or a miso-based condiment. The grilling and glaz-ing can continue for some time, until the *onigiri* are deep brown or the aroma drives the hungry diner to interrupt the process.

The most common grilled vegetable is likely *nasu*, or eggplant, as, skin and all, it is placed on the yakiami. When the skin is black and wrinkled, the eggplant is removed to a cutting board to be peeled. The flesh is then separated by hand into strips, which may then be mixed with *dashi* and grated ginger, and often served chilled. At other times, the eggplant is halved and thickly coated with a sweetened miso paste and returned to the grill until small bubbles form in the miso. Today, these high-quality grills are mostly made by craftspeople in the Kansai area.

A lid is a lid is a lid. Well, not in Japan. *Otoshi-buta*, or drop lids, have a unique use. The light discs of hinoki, which have tapered edges and are smaller in diameter than the pot, float on top of liquids as they simmer. The function is to ensure that heat is distributed evenly and to prevent roiling bubbles. This reduces the mechanical stress on the food and keeps fragile materials in their original shape.

And here's a chef's secret. Since the lids are untreated wood they must be soaked in water for a few minutes prior to use to avoid absorbing the flavor of the dish and tainting the flavor of the next liquid to be simmered. And this advice from a friend who's an architect and a dedicated cook: Look for quality lids. The grips of the less expensive ones tend to be glued in, as opposed to being slotted in with no adhesives or nails. After repeated simmering sessions, the glue can also taint the flavor of the food.

Like the cuisine, many Japanese cooking brushes, or **hake**, are handmade by skilled artisans using "recipes" handed down through generations. The brushes are used to coat fish, tofu or *yakitori* chicken skewers with sauces. They're also used to dust food with flour, such as small horse mackerel for deep frying and tofu for *agedashidofu*.

In fine sushi shops, the head chef, or *oyakata*, will keep two separate containers with brushes. The brushes of one will be used for lightly lacing *nigi-rizushi* sushi pieces with soy sauce; the other for the rich and sweet *anago* sauce. There are many types of sauce, known as *tare*, but all have soy sauce

as a base. Teriyaki tare, for example, is made of light soy sauce, *mirin* (brown sugar can be substituted) and sake. The thicker tare for anago is sake, brown sugar, mirin, soy sauce and *tamari* soy sauce.

The bristles are usually made of horse hair or sheep's wool, and often bound at the handle with copper. The white brushes are made from sheep's wool, spun into threads. These refined, soft brushes are used to dress delicate food items. The brushes can easily be cleaned in hot water. Though plastic-handled brushes are available, chef friends insist wooden handles are stronger and last longer.

Every kitchen is home to several pairs of *saibashi*, or cooking chopsticks, and they usually come with various degrees of burns and wear. The biggest difference from chopsticks used for dining is their length—the bamboo or cypress utensils are usually more than twelve inches long, making them handy for shifting food items or plucking them from hot water or oil.

To save their wooden saibashi from absorbing oil, however, many cooks will keep on hand a metal-tipped pair, for handling tempura, *tonkatsu* and other fried dishes.

Saibashi usually come tied together at their tops with coarse string, to keep them together on the journey from workshop or factory to store and home. Most people remove the string or replace it with a soft thread of cotton. And though wooden saibashi become charred and misshapen through long use, there will always be a favorite pair which the owner is reluctant to part with.

Journalist, 31
Two-person household
LENGTH: 12¾"

Caregiver for Elderly, mid 40s
Two-person household
L: 12"

Fashion model, 29
Two-person household
L: 12⅞"

Veterinarian and mother, 40-something
Four-person household
L: 13⅛"

Bank Teller and mother, 40-something
Five-person household
L: 10½"

Voice Actor/Narrator, 53
Single household
L: 12⅞"

This handmade bamboo colander is elegant from any angle, but from the top it is especially attractive. Though not an everyday tool for most households, the **shikizaru**, or *nizaru*, can be used in the making of *tsukudani*, a garnish made of either fish, *konbu* seaweed or meat, simmered in soy sauce and *mirin* rice sherry, and eaten with rice. But the utensil's most common application is in fine *kappo* or *ryotei* cooking, where it simmers fragile foods such as fish, especially sea bream. In a cuisine in which presentation is as important as taste, the shikizaru's delicacy is crucial: a cooked whole fish must be just that—chefs want to avoid even the tiniest tear in the skin or loss of flesh during cooking.

In practice, the shikizaru is placed in the bottom of a pot with the food arranged on top. Using the "handles," the cook can move the food during simmering without risk of disfiguration or sticking.

Though the shikizaru's life-span is short—probably around twenty uses—these utensils are meticulously constructed, a testament to the refinement of Japanese craftsmanship, even when it comes to disposable items.

Uragoshi are traditional Japanese sieves. This fetching example is made of cypress and, like the *waseiro* steamer, is tied with strong cherry tree bark. Its very fine mesh is tautly woven horsehair. Uragoshi are especially convenient to use because they rest solidly on mixing bowls and pots.

So, what sort of materials are processed with one of these sieves? Today many cooks use them to create Western recipes, such as a smooth potage. Or to remove the thin skins of egg yolk. But their most likely application is with ingredients for Japanese sweets: for starches such as *kuzuko* (from the root of kudzu vine) and *kanten* (agar), which are pushed through the fine mesh. *Yokan* and other desserts use cooked *azuki* beans, chestnuts and *satsu-maimo*, a Japanese yam.

Kurikinton, made with yam and chestnut, is commonly made at home. The still-warm nut meat and sweet potato are placed on the uragoshi and, with a scraping motion, are mashed through the sieve with a *shamoji* or *hera*. The result is the finest texture possible—one of the most desirable qualities for the Japanese palate.

The Presentation

Moritsuke, or presentation, is undoubtedly the most challenging aspect of Japanese cooking. Since the cuisine is meant to appeal to the five senses—elevating visual effect to an art form—how a meal is arranged is as important as the choice of tableware. Since time is crucial in serving, presentation must be executed swiftly.

To save time, the cook will likely decide upon the serving vessels in advance, matching food and tableware according to color, texture and the seasons.

The cook rapidly, but meticulously, arranges food on these carefully chosen pieces. In a matter of seconds, fingers will have deftly formed grated *daikon* radish into a mound and placed it next to a grilled fish; then with sharply pointed chopsticks positioned thinly sliced pieces of *yuzu* (a fragrant citrus) peel onto the radish. Fresh *wasabi* will be grated and primped with the fingers into a wee cone to crown the top of a square of cold tofu. Swiftly, the cook moves on to the next plate.

Imagine having this individual grater, or *yakumi oroshigane*, topped with a stick of fresh wasabi, brought to your table so that you might grate relish for your soba noodles. While the craftsman took great care with the aesthetics (making this is a most covetable object!), he also considered the diner's comfort. The handcrafted, tin-coated copper crane, which symbolizes good luck and long life, is designed to nestle in the palm of the hand, making grating much easier than if it were the standard utensil, which is held by the end.

From the same craftsman as the "crane" grater opposite, form and function also abound in this turtle: its head raised as a grip for the user, its tail serving as a loop for hanging in the kitchen. These graters embody the spirit of *omotenashi*—the idea of gracious hospitality carried out effortlessly. It's no coincidence that the craftsman chose these two animals. The crane is said to live a thousand years, the turtle ten thousand. Representing both long and prosperous lives, they are often used as symbols on celebratory occasions.

This **chirirenge**, a slotted ladle of pounded bronze, is used traditionally in nabe dishes. The perforations make it perfect for draining excess soup, which would dilute the dipping sauce, when lifting tofu and vegetables. The design of the chirirenge differs from the *otama* or *shakushi*. It is based on Chinese ladles, called *renge* for the lotus flower. The shape of the spoon head is said to look like the petal of a fallen ("*chiri*") lotus flower. The curved handle is also typical of Chinese spoons.

Few craftsmen work in bronze, as it is both expensive and difficult to form. The use of bronze in this chirirenge is purely an aesthetic conceit, and though it dazzles the eye, another version comes with even more flair—the perforations are in the shape of cherry blossoms. Of course, such extravagance would rarely be seen in the kitchen. More likely at the table, serving lucky diners.

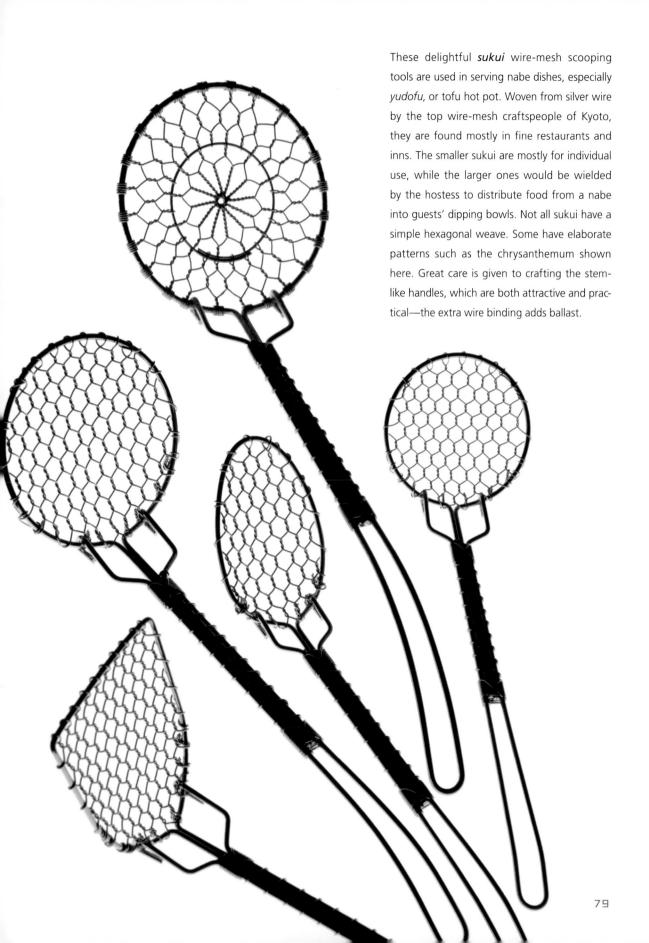

These delightful *sukui* wire-mesh scooping tools are used in serving nabe dishes, especially *yudofu*, or tofu hot pot. Woven from silver wire by the top wire-mesh craftspeople of Kyoto, they are found mostly in fine restaurants and inns. The smaller sukui are mostly for individual use, while the larger ones would be wielded by the hostess to distribute food from a nabe into guests' dipping bowls. Not all sukui have a simple hexagonal weave. Some have elaborate patterns such as the chrysanthemum shown here. Great care is given to crafting the stem-like handles, which are both attractive and practical—the extra wire binding adds ballast.

"To be honest, the art of *moritsuke* is probably taken to its highest form in *kappo* and *kaiseki* places. After all, those chefs must work with so many different ingredients, colors and textures, arranging several plates in the course of a meal.

But in my world, the sushi world, we work with limited materials—seafood and garnishes such as shredded *daikon*, *shiso* leaves and grated wasabi. And most chefs pretty much conform to a set pattern for arranging the items on a ceramic plate or wooden tray. No one tells you how to do it; I learned years ago as an apprentice at Kyubei by closely observing the *oyakata* and then practicing endlessly until I got the hang of it.

Most sushi chefs use metal-tipped moritsukebashi, because the odor of fish clings to wooden ones. So, moritsuke in sushi shops is basic. While admittedly the shape of the *nigiri*, and the balance between the *neta* (topping) and rice, is important, the final result is simply placed in front of the customers. But sashimi requires a more complicated presentation. Many of my regulars like to linger over their meal, starting with beer and sashimi, working their way slowly to nigiri. With sashimi, two or three types of seasonal fish are often presented on one plate. So I use shredded radish to prop up the slices, shiso leaves to separate fish types and even little flowers.

But sometimes, it is enough to just take advantage of the material at hand. Take *uni*, or sea urchin, for example. When it is in season, I can simply present a halved uni in a glass bowl. The spiny black shell and orange flesh are such a beautiful combination that it's an artistic collaboration with nature. Come to think of it, moritsuke in the sushi world is all about the fish . . . and how it is cut. It's very basic and elemental, true, but the way the fish is cut is everything."

Makoto Yokoshima

Chef
Koshiki

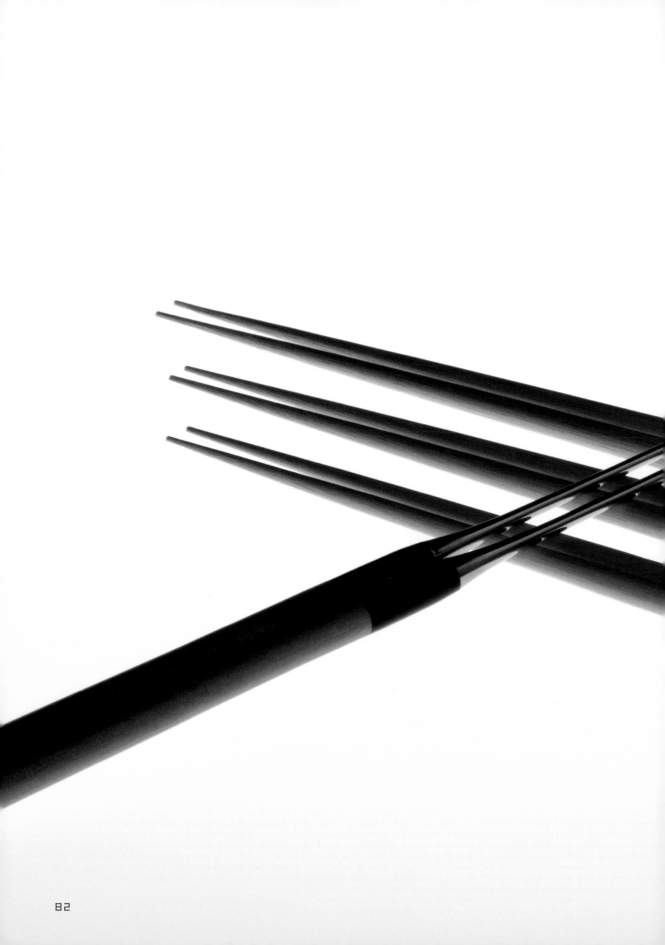

Japanese cuisine is meant to stimulate all five senses, and the use of these *moritsuke-bashi* chopsticks for presentation and arrangement are essential to the culture. They help cooks skillfully arrange food, garnishes and other adornments—such as a tiny maple leaf—on tableware chosen for the food and the occasion.

Like the *saibashi* utensils used in cooking, moritsuke-bashi are longer than those used by diners. However, they differ in two ways. First, they tend to be more elegantly constructed, since they are also used to serve from bowls of food to be shared. Secondly, the tips of moritsuke-bashi, whether metal, bamboo or wood, are tapered to very fine, almost weapon-like points, allowing the chef to place and arrange the most delicate of food items and tiny garnishes. If one were to relate the art of cooking to painting, these chopsticks would be the detail brushes.

There is something symbolic about the *shamoji* rice server, which looks like a rounded paddle, probably because it always appears with steamed rice, the most important component of a Japanese meal (the word *gohan* means both "meal" and "rice"). The shamoji is used when serving rice from the cooker, a task which, prior to the spread of Western furniture, was performed on tatami, at low tables called *chabudai*. Shamoji are also used to gently fold vinegar into sushi rice, so as not to damage the grain. A metal utensil would not only cut through the grains, but rice would stick to it, making scooping difficult. As long as it is dipped in water before use, rice slides easily from a wooden shamoji.

Traditional shamoji come in various shapes and woods, including zelkova, magnolia and cypress, as well as bamboo. The different wood types offer a range of colors and textures, while on some finely crafted shamoji, the handle may be carved thicker than the blade, providing a comfortable grip.

For serving at the table, a lacquered shamoji may be preferred, though these days, most people have taken to using plastic ones. The latest plastic shamoji have a dimpled surface, making them virtually non-stick.

Still, most cooks will retain at least an inexpensive bamboo shamoji, and the wooden version remains the preferred tool for stirring fried rice

Shamoji purportedly have talismanic qualities. They are sometimes called *mijima*, after Miyajima Island near Hiroshima—home to one of Japan's most famous shrines. A Shinto priest there, who lamented the lack of souvenir items at his shrine, had a dream about the goddess of art and love, Benten. The goddess plays the *biwa*, a kind of lute, and the priest saw his dream as a sign to make a rice scoop based on the instrument's shape. People came from all over Japan, embracing the mijima as an object that scooped up good luck . . . and the shrine's fortunes were assured. These shamoji range in size from about six to twelve inches.

Jewelry Designer/Shop owner, 36
Two-person household
LENGTH: 10¼"

Restaurant owner, 40s
Two-person household
L: 9½"

Taxi driver, 38
One-person household
L: 8⅔"

Bank Teller and mother, 40-something
Four-person household
L: 8¼"

Housewife and mother, 53
Four-person household
L: 8½"

Grandmother, 87
Two-person household
L: 6½"

The *handai*, also called a *hangiri* or *sushi oke*, is the round, flat-bottomed wooden tub or barrel used in the last stage of making sushi rice, or to serve rice for *temaki* (do-it-yourself) *sushi*. After the rice has been cooked, it is gently shifted to a tub that has been soaked for a while in water to prevent sticking, and spread across the bottom. Care is taken to move the rice in as few motions as possible, so as to avoid disfiguration. The dimensions of the handai work to help set the rice, as moisture evaporates quickly from the vessel's broad surface area.

These tubs are traditionally made of *hinoki* or *sawara*—both varieties of cypress. The one pictured here is handmade of sawara, preferred by some cooks over hinoki as it is not as strong-scented. A hint of cypress may be welcome but it should not overpower the food.

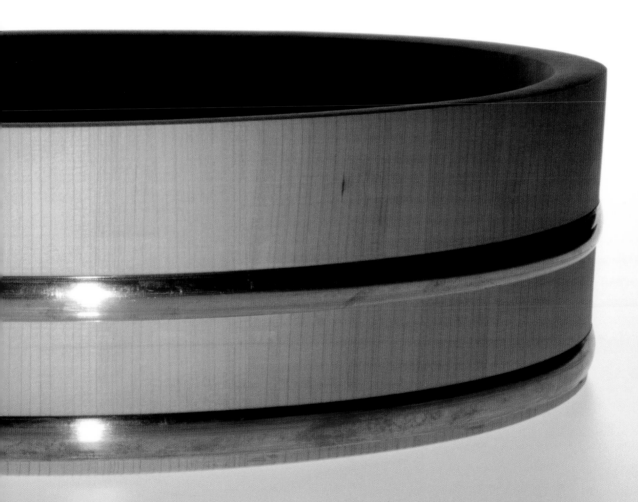

This elegant steamed-rice tub, or **ohitsu**, is made of *sawara* cypress, and is used to keep rice warm at the table. The sawara comes from the forests of Kiso in Nagano prefecture, and is rated so highly that it is protected by the government. In fact, the shrines at the sacred Ise complex, one of Japan's most revered sites, are ritually rebuilt in twenty-year cycles, using Kiso sawara.

Traditionally, rice would be transferred from a cooker to an ohitsu and placed at the edge of a low table on the *tatami*, where the housewife would sit. It was her job to dish the rice into family members' bowls and replenish them.

Today, as busy schedules mean that families rarely share their mealtimes, we often see family members serving themselves directly from the rice cooker. It's more likely that ohitsu only make an appearance on special occasions or when entertaining guests. I've even seen one creative hostess using ohitsu small enough to hold only one or two portions of rice, for individual place settings.

While most ohitsu today are made by machine, this vessel was made entirely by hand using a round plane. It took more than eight hours to finish.

Makisu mats are essential in the making of *makizushi* sushi rolls, and tend to be the same size—ten inches square. It may look like a snap in the hands of a seasoned cook, but making sushi rolls is far from easy. The *nori* seaweed is laid on the mat, then coated with vinegared sushi rice and filling before being rolled. But without years of practice, spreading the rice evenly and rolling it in a smooth, even motion to create an aesthetically pleasing spiral of filling can be maddeningly frustrating.

Makisu have long been used to shape other items as well, such as omelets, or to squeeze off excess liquid from food materials. One friend, for example, uses hers to strain off the last traces of water from spinach while shaping it for *ohitashi*. For this dish, spinach is cooked whole, with the ends dipped in the boiling water first before the leaves are plunged. While the spinach is still firm, it is removed and squeezed into a tight roll before slicing.

Curiously, the origin of these delightful wooden rice molds, or ***mosso-ki*** is found in the austere world of Buddhist temples. When priests gathered for special occasions, monks had difficulty figuring out how to serve rice to so many diners at once. So, the rice mold was concocted to press and cut out the rice into shapes that could easily be provided *en masse*.

Ryotei, the finest Japanese restaurants, took the mosso-ki to another level, adding more shapes, including plums, pines and bamboo. It should be noted, however, that at such restaurants the pressed rice would not be served at the meal proper but more likely given out later in bento boxes as gifts.

The wooden mold must be soaked before use to avoid sticking. For a dish called "cut rice," steamed white rice or *okowa* (a combination of regular rice and sticky rice mixed with small bits of vegetables or chicken) is put in the box, pressed, and cleanly cut to make even shapes. Incidentally, the molds used to fashion Japanese *wagashi* sweets look very much the same as mosso-ki.

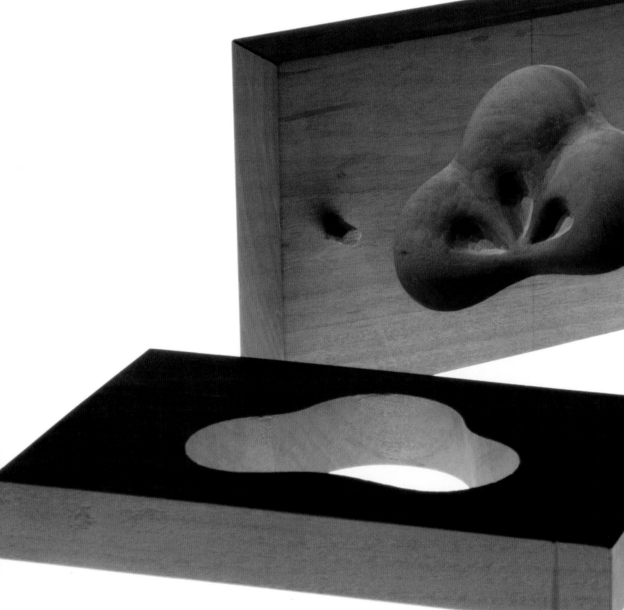

Want to impress friends with your perfectly formed rice sculptures? Invest in *onigiri* rice-ball molds, *onigiriki*, and pressed sushi molds. In the Japanese home, the onigiriki would be used for parties or to prepare bento boxes for other festive occasions, such as cherry blossom viewing or a day at the *kabuki* theater. A relatively modern convenience—probably developed in the early twentieth century—even these wooden models are becoming more rare: these days, many people use plastic onigiriki.

Oshizushi or pressed sushi, which originated in the western Kansai region, is easy to make when you have a tool such as this (below). It has three parts: the rectangular wall and top and bottom pieces that fit just inside. The bottom and wall are immersed in water before use so that rice won't stick to the surfaces. The bottom is set into the wall, and sushi rice is added, along with a topping such as pickled *saba* mackerel. Then the top is used to press down the materials, packing the rice and topping into a firm but light "brick." Hold the top down with one hand and lift the wall, then remove the top for slicing.

Several friends from Osaka and Kyoto told me they were homesick upon seeing this photo, since **oshizushiki** remain widely used only in those areas.

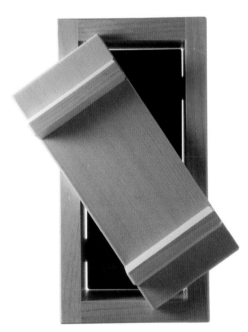

Cleaning Up

The compact dimensions of the Japanese kitchen and the fact that most lack automatic dishwashers mean that cooks must be efficient at cleaning up as they move through their work, even from the preparation stage. In fact, by the time a meal is served the kitchen is often spotless. Knives have been washed, dried and put away. The cutting board has been scrubbed down with a *tawashi* brush (detergents should never be used as the wood absorbs them, tainting the next item to be chopped), wiped down and set upright to dry. The grater, which has been soaked in water, is scraped to remove ginger fibers.

Every chef knows a number of tricks to remove the smells that cling to what are largely organic tools. To remove the fishy scent from a *donabe* clay hotpot, for instance, one can fill it with boiling water and toss in a teaspoon of green tea leaves.

At any rate, a chef can only join diners at the table knowing the kitchen is shipshape.

When it's time to clean-up, the Japanese kitchen bristles with handy gadgets, the most common being the *tawashi*, a horse-shoe-shaped, all-purpose scrubber made of palm (far right). But there are highly special-ized cleaners, too. Ever wondered how to reach the bottom when cleaning your *tok-kuri* sake server? Enter the **tokkuri arai**, or sake server cleaner. The pale, white cotton-bound brush has a long handle that extends deep inside the server. How about cleaning *zaru* or strainers? If you've ever strained bonito flakes after making soup stock, you'll know they are almost impossible to wash off with ease. It's best to leave the strainer and residual flakes to dry, then scrub with the **seiro arai**. With this sturdy brush—three columns of bundled palm strands bound with copper wire—the flakes fall right off. Harried dishwashers will also appreciate the double-headed wire brush for cleaning tea pots, which looks a little Western in style, and the broom-like brush for whisking flour from a counter or cutting board. For washing fine utensils, such as copper or brass pots, there is the **karukaya tawashi**. This lighter colored plant-material brush is gentle on surfaces but effective in removing grease.

With the increase of cooks who are envi-ronmentally aware, these all-natural brushes are enjoying a comeback.

Fukin, or wiping cloths made of cotton, silk, linen or hemp, are ever-present in professional and private kitchens. This one is a classic *sarashi* of bleached silk (though sarashi can also be made of cotton). It is the preferred cloth of chefs, who use the billowy tissues to dry knives after each use, as well as for wiping down *manaita* cutting boards. At home sarashi are used to dry fine pottery and clean surfaces, and to cover leftover rice, helping to retain moisture before the rice is used in a fried rice dish—or for rice gruel or rice balls. The roots of the sarashi are in the Shinto religion, where white represents purity.

Fukin are absorbent, wash out easily and dry quickly. Many are still handspun, following Japan's rich tradition of weaving.

Odds & Ends

Most cooks could get by without these bits and bobs. But who wouldn't want them? They have traditional uses, but it is certainly fun to think of new applications. I've seen bamboo mini tongs used for serving ice cubes or chunks of brown sugar for espresso. And the conventionally shaped bamboo whisk and the cherry fruit whisk are small enough to mix cocktails. But the prong, called a *tofu sashi*, is still at its handiest when employed to spear tofu from a simmering dish of *yudofu* or *nabemono*.

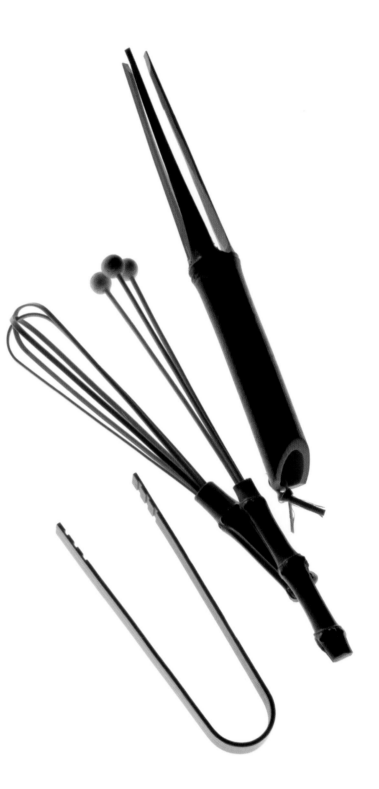

Sharpening stones, or *toishi*, are indispensable for anyone with Japanese knives—which are made of carbon (not stainless) steel. Though knives in the average home kitchen are sharpened once every few months, no professional would let a day pass without putting blade to stone.

Natural water stones are still found in Japan, but are extremely expensive and only used by professionals (a brick-size stone ranges between three hundred to three thousand US dollars). So those made of alumina, such as these on the left, suffice for most kitchens. The serious sharpener will have on hand three types: The *Ara-to* (rough) has a rough surface and is used in the first stage of sharpening, as well as in repairing chips or broken tips. It is also used to reshape the knife's pitch angle, for a sharper blade. The *Naka-to* (medium rough) is used after the ara-to to make the blade even sharper. Finally, the *Shiage-to*, or finishing stone, is employed to finish off the sharpening process.

The less serious sharpener will make do with just the medium stone, but the process is the same. First the stone is submerged in water for five minutes or so to remove air from inside. The stone is placed on a cloth and the blade is drawn over it at an angle of 10 to 15 degrees with lengthwise or circular movements under gentle pressure. The most important point in knife sharpening is keeping the pitch angle—unlike the blades of Western knives, which are angled equally on both sides, Japanese blades are pitched more sharply on one side than the other.

The white *kappo-gi*, or "cook's wear," is the standard chef's uniform. For people of a certain age, it conjures the image of their mother, bustling through the kitchen, the smock draped over her kimono.

The term "*kappo*" is fairly new, probably originating in the mid-19th century, and is written with the characters for "*ka*" (meaning to cut) and "*po*" (meaning to simmer), a fair summation of the act of cooking. Today, to speak of a "kappo restaurant" refers to a very refined eatery. The kappo-gi itself debuted at Japan's first culinary academy, which opened in Nihonbashi in Tokyo in 1882. In those days, most people wore kimono on a daily basis, though the affluent classes had begun to appear in the recently introduced Western suits and dresses.

What sets the kappogi apart from the apron is that it was devised with kimono wear in mind. The long, open sleeves of a kimono can be held up by ties in the smock, allowing the cook to move comfortably about the kitchen without, say, worrying about dragging the sleeves through a just-prepared dish. Eventually, though, many cooks stopped wearing kimono in the kitchen. Today, though kappogi with ties for the kimono sleeves are sold, most are bound at the wrists by elastic. These are most commonly worn with loose pants and caps.

Footwear has not changed, however. The wooden clogs, called *geta*, are still the preferred gear for the tradition-conscious chef, though a few sport straw geta instead. The geta can be worn with or without *tabi*—split-toed socks—though in colder climes tabi are commonly worn. Many fine restaurants have slate or concrete kitchen floors; immaculate surfaces which can easily be hosed and scrubbed down. Just the clack-clack of the wooden geta on stone will make customers' mouths water for the meal to come.

Stocking Your Kitchen

So where do I find these wonderful tools, and satisfy my collecting habit? Straight off, Aritsugu of Kyoto and Kiya of Tokyo, the two major cooking utensil purveyors of Japan, and providers of the majority of beautiful tools we've featured in this book. Aritsugu has been selling knives and other tools for more than 400 years; Kiya for more than 200. Of course, Japan has many small specialty shops such as Tokyo's Beniya Mingeiten and Takumi, both specializing in folk craft. There, you'll find bamboo strainers, mortars and cooking chopsticks, alongside their non-kitchen goods.

If you've got time to poke around Kappabashi, Tokyo's "Bowery" restaurant supply district, you'll find all you need for your Japanese kitchen toolkit and more (they stock Chinese, French and Italian tools, too). Tokyu Hands, the do-it-yourself stores, carry a selection of domestic utensils, as do fine departments stores. So while the following list is certainly incomplete, it may at least help you begin stocking your cupboards with the basics for cooking Japanese cuisine.

The Restaurants

Tokyo is chockablock with fantastic restaurants. I asked the chefs at a few of my personal favorites to provide "illustrations" of how a few tools are used in three stages of food preparation.

Pages 22 & 23

Friend Toshio Tanahashi creates *Shojin*, which is the vegetarian cuisine of Zen temples, in his sanctuary in central Tokyo. Tanahashi-san studied for four years at a nunnery renowned for its excellent Shojin, and at his place he will both serve the standard—such as *gomadofu*—and experiment in his ten-plus course meal, featuring up to forty vegetables.

Gesshinkyo   4-24-12 Jingumae, Shibuya-ku   Tel. 03-3796-6575

Pages 58 & 59

Waketokuyama is sublime. Chef Nozaki-san, who also teaches cooking and writes prolifically on food, serves ultra refined Japanese cuisine that manages to never be fancy or prententious. His broths and sauces are very subtle, allowing the fresh ingredients to show off their true flavor. The senses are elevated on every level at Waketokuyama—it was even designed by noted architect Kengo Kuma.

Waketokuyama
5-1-5 Minami-Azabu, Minato-ku   Tel.03-5789-3838

Pages 80 & 81

Sushi devotees tend to have their favorite shops, where they know the *oyakata* and the prices (fine sushi restaurants post no menus). For me, it's my neighborhood haunt, Koshiki, where professors from a nearby university strike up conversations with, say, a has-been chanteuse and the head of the Tsukiji fish market union.

Koshiki   2-11-6 Shirokanedai, Minato-ku   Tel.03-3280-0203

The Shops

Aritsugu has been in the business since 1560, selling knives, pots, ladles and other tools to professional chefs.
219 Kajiya-cho, Gokomachi Nishiiru Nishikikouji,
Nakagyou-ku, Kyoto
Phone: 075-221-1095 Fax: 075-231-1066
www.aritsugu.com (in Japanese, and some English)

Kiya has been in the kitchen tool business since 1792, selling knives, pots, ladles and other tools to professional chefs.
Main store
1-5-6 Nihonbashi-Muromachi, Chuo-ku, Tokyo
Phone: 03-3241-0010 Fax: 03-3241-0618
www.kiya-hamono.co.jp (Japanese and some English)

Beniya Mingeiten sells a wide range of handmade bamboo crafts from strainers and cooking chopsticks to tongs and egg-beaters. It also carries lovely mortars and pestles and ohitsu rice tubs.
Puremu Aoyama
4-20-19 Minami-Aoyama, Minato-ku, Tokyo
Phone: 03-3403-8115 Fax: 03-3403-8124
beniya.m78.com

Takumi has been selling a wide range of crafts, including pottery, lacquer ware and bamboo since 1933.
8-4-2 Ginza, Chuo-Ku, Tokyo, Phone: 03-3571-2017
www.ginza-takumi.co.jp (Japanese only)

Oyaseisakujo handcrafts copper *oroshigane* graters, including the distinctive crane and turtle (pages 76-77). You can find Mr. Oya's work at Kiya, or at his workshop in Saitama, north of Tokyo.
2-6-1 Chuo, Wako City, Saitama Prefecture
Phone: 048-464-3705 Fax: 048-464-7068
www.amoju.com/oroshi/ (Japanese only)

Tokyu Hands Shibuya sells just about everything, including Japanese kitchen tools.
12-18 Udagawa-cho, Shibuya-ku, Tokyo   Phone: 03-5489-5111
www.tokyu-hands.co.jp (Japanese only)

Nagatani Seito is a maker of the ceramic nabe and grills from the Iga kilns in Mie prefecture and runs a showroom in central Tokyo. Besides the nabe pots, the igamono line features plates, tea pots, ceramic beer mugs and more.
1-22-27 Ebisu, Shibuya-ku, Tokyo
Phone: 03-3440-7071 Fax.3440-7041
www.igamono.co.jp (Japanese only)

Kame no Ko sells all types of handmade cleaning up brushes.
6-14-8 Takinogawa, Kita-ku, Tokyo
Phone: 03-3916-3231 Fax: 03-3916-5959
www.kamenoko-tawashi.co.jp (in Japanese only)

Fujimoto Tora sells handmade cooking brushes and cleaning up brushes.
2-19-4 Kaminarimon, Taito-ku, Tokyo
Phone: 03-5828-1818 Fax: 03-5828-2218

Nakagawa Seichichi Shoten sells elegant *fukin* or cleaning up cloths spun of linen, silk and cotton.
178-2 Ikeda machi, Nara City, Nara Prefecture
Phone: 0742-61-6676 Fax: 0742-61-6672
www.yu-nakagawa.co.jp/ (in Japanese only)
Tokyo Showroom
Maison 115, 1-15-4 Ebisu, Shibuya-ku, Tokyo
Phone: 03-5789-3228 Fax: 03-578-3226

Ichihara Heibei Shoten sells bamboo chopsticks, including pairs made from the rafters of old Japanese farmhouses.
Shimogyoku, Sakaimachi Dori, Shijosagaru, Kyoto
Phone: 075-341-3831 Fax: 075-341-3832

Kappabashi features an endless number of stalls and stores selling supplies to restaurants, from fake food models to kitchen appliances and tools.
Closest station:Tawaramachi (Ginza subway line)
www.kappabashi.or.jp/ (Japanese only)

Tokifusa Iizuka's gorgeous knives can be purchased online in the at the following site:
www.bladegallery.com/knives/maker.asp?code=188&display=Tokifusa+Iizuka

The Items

Title Page

ENGLISH NAME: Ohitsu set
JAPANESE NAME: おひつセット
ROMANIZED JAPANESE: *Ohitsu setto*
SIZE: 5-*go*/五合/5 cups
SHOP: Kiya

Pages 12 & 13

Sashimi knife 柳刃 *Yanagi-ba*
Blade: $10\frac{1}{2}$" Handle: $5\frac{1}{2}$"
Kiya/Sold under the tradename,
Shigefusa

Broad-bladed knife for fish
and meat
出刃包丁 *Deba-bocho*
Blade: $6\frac{1}{2}$" Handle: 5"
Kiya/Sold under the tradename,
Shigefusa 重房作

Page 14

Broad-bladed knife for fish
and meat
團十郎出刃 包丁
Danjuro Deba-bocho
Blade: 6" Handle: $4\frac{7}{8}$"
Kiya

Page 15

Noodle-cutting knife
麺切 包丁 *Menkiri-bocho*
Blade: $9\frac{1}{2}$"
Kiya

Pages 16 & 17 (FROM TOP)

Sashimi knife 柳刃 *Yanagi-ba*
Blade: $9\frac{1}{2}$" Handle: $5\frac{1}{3}$"
Aritsugu

Sashimi knife (Kansai-style)
柳刃 *Yanagi-ba*
Blade: 13" Handle: 6"
Kiya

Sashimi knife (Kanto-style)
柳刃/蛸引 *Yanagi-ba./takobiki*
Blade: $10\frac{1}{2}$" Handle: $5\frac{1}{3}$"
Kiya/sold under the tradename,
Shigefusa 重房作

Page 18

Vegetable knife
全印菜包丁 *Nakiri-bocho*
Blade: 6" Handle: $4\frac{1}{2}$"
Kiya

Page 19

Vegetable knife
薄切 *Usugiri-bocho*

Blade: $8\frac{1}{4}$" Handle: $5\frac{1}{2}$"
Kiya

Pages 20 & 21

The Five Basic Knives
家庭用基本一式
Katei you kihon isshiki
Aritsugu

Petty knife
上製ペテイナイフ *Josei Peti Naifu*
L: $4\frac{1}{8}$"

Sashimi knife
柳刃上製刺身包丁 *Yanagi-ba*
Blade: $8\frac{1}{4}$" Handle: $4\frac{7}{8}$"

Broad-bladed knife
登録出刃 *Toroku Deba*
Blade: 7" Handle: $5\frac{1}{4}$"

Multi-purpose kitchen knife
上製三徳包丁 *Josei Santoku-bocho*
Blade: 7" Handle: $4\frac{1}{2}$"

Vegetable knife
登録鎌型薄刃
Toroku Kamagata Usuba
Blade: 6" Handle: $4\frac{3}{4}$"

Pages 24 & 25

Mortar すり鉢 *Suribachi*
D: $12\frac{3}{8}$" H: $5\frac{3}{8}$"
Beniya Mingeiten

Pepper tree Pestle
山椒すりこぎ *Sansho Surikogi*
L: $14\frac{3}{8}$"
Beniya Mingeiten

Page 26

Mortar すり鉢 *Suribachi*
D: $8\frac{1}{2}$" H: $5\frac{1}{4}$"
Beniya Mingeiten

Page 27 (FROM TOP)

Sesame Toaster
胡麻いり *Goma iri*
L, including handle: $7\frac{3}{8}$"
W: 4" H: $1\frac{1}{3}$"
Aritsugu

Gingko nut toaster
銀杏いり *Ginan-iri*
L, including handle: $17\frac{1}{8}$"
D: $9\frac{1}{3}$" H: 2"
Aritsugu

Sesame Toaster
胡麻いり *Goma iri*
L, including handle: $8\frac{1}{4}$"

D: $4\frac{3}{4}$" H: $2\frac{2}{3}$"
Takumi

Page 28

Copper Grater
銅おろし金 *Do Oroshigane*
L: $8\frac{1}{8}$" W: $4\frac{3}{8}$"
Oyaseisakujo

Page 29

Sharkskin covered grater
さめ皮おろし金
Samekawa Oroshigane
L: $5\frac{1}{4}$" W: $3\frac{1}{4}$"
Kiya

Page 30

"Devil's Grater"
鬼おろし *Oni Oroshi*
L: $11\frac{1}{4}$" W: $3\frac{1}{4}$" H: $1\frac{1}{2}$"
Beniya Mingeiten

Page 31

Bonito Shaving Tool
鰹削り器 *Katsuokezuriki*
L. with lid: 10" W: 4"
Aritsugu

Pages 32 & 33

7 Stacking pans
七枚組鍋 *Nanamai-kumi-nabe*
(SMALL TO LARGE)
D: $6\frac{1}{8}$", H: 3"
D: 7", H: $3\frac{1}{4}$"
D: $7\frac{3}{4}$", H: $3\frac{1}{2}$"
D: $8\frac{1}{3}$", H: $3\frac{2}{3}$"
D: $9\frac{1}{3}$", H: $4\frac{1}{2}$"
D: 10", H: 5"
D: $10\frac{3}{4}$", H: $5\frac{1}{4}$"
Aritsugu

Pan Grip 鍋矢床 *Nabe Yattoko*
L: $8\frac{7}{8}$"
Aritsugu

Page 34

Pan 行平鍋 *Yukihiranabe*
L: 7" H: $2\frac{7}{8}$"
Volume: $1\frac{1}{2}$ quarts
Aritsugu

Pages 36 & 37

Bamboo Strainers ざる *Zaru*
L to R

Rice Strainer
米揚げざる *Komeage zaru*
D: 13" H: 6"
Kiya

Tray sieve 盆ざる *Bonzaru*
D: $11\frac{7}{8}$" H: 3"
Kiya

Tray sieve 盆ざる *Bonzaru*
D: 7" H: $1\frac{1}{8}$"
Beniya Mingeiten

Hexagonal weave basket
六ツ目かご *Mutsume kago*
D: $6\frac{7}{8}$" H: $2\frac{1}{8}$"
Beniya Mingeiten

Strainer ladle with leg Beniya
足付お玉ざる *Ashizukiotamazaru*
D: 5" H: 2" L: $5\frac{3}{4}$"
Beniya Mingeiten

Tea strainer
竹茶こし *Takechakoshi*
D: $2\frac{1}{2}$" H: $3\frac{1}{8}$" L: $6\frac{1}{3}$"
Beniya Mingeiten

Tray sieve 盆ざる *Bonzaru*
Beniya Mingeiten

Page 38

Strainer ladle with hand
手付お玉ざる *Tetsuke-otama zaru.*
D: $5\frac{1}{8}$" H: 3"
Beniya Mingeiten

Page 39

Soba basket with base
そばざる *(台付き)*
Soba zaru (dai tsuki)
D: $8\frac{7}{8}$" H: $2\frac{3}{4}$"
Takumi

Pages 40 & 41 (FROM LEFT)

Vegetable cutters
野菜抜形 *Yasai nuki kata*

Gingko tree leaf
いちょう *Itcho*
W: $1\frac{1}{3}$" H: $2\frac{1}{8}$"
Aritsugu

Maple leaf 紅葉 *Momiji*
H: $1\frac{1}{3}$"
Aritsugu

Plum leaf 梅 *Ume*
W: $1\frac{1}{8}$" H: $2\frac{1}{8}$"
Aritsugu

Fish Deboner—Kanto style
骨抜き (関東形) *Hone nuki*
$4\frac{3}{4}$"
Aritsugu

Oyster opener
カキむき *Kakimuki*
Diameter: $7\frac{2}{3}$"
Aritsugu

Scale remover
うろことり *Urokotori*

H: 7¼"
Aritsugu

Scraper/Convenient Brush
すくれば（便利はけ）
Sukureepa (Benri Hake)
H: 5⅓"
Beniya Mingeiten

Kushi Skewers

Grilled Chicken Skewer
焼き鳥串　*Yakitori Kushi*
H: 5⅞"
Kiya

Tofu Skewer
田楽串　*Dengaku Kushi*
H: 5⅞"
Kiya

Skewer　鉄砲串　*Teppokushi*
H: 5⅞"
Kiya

Knotted Skewer
むすび串　*Musubi Kushi*
H: 4½"
Kiya

Pages 44 & 45
Rice Cooker (3 portions)
飯釜（3合）*Okama (3 go)*
Diameter: 7⅞"　H: 8¼"
Takumi

Pages 46 & 47
Cover/Japanese steamer
釜蓋／和蒸籠　*Kamabuta/Waseiro*
Lid Diameter: 10½" x H: 3½"
Steamer Diameter: 8⅞" x H: 5⅞"
Kiya

Pages 48 & 49
Ceramic pot (Iga kiln)
土鍋　*Donabe*
Diameter: 12½"　H: 8⅞"
Nagatani Ceramics/
Igamono Line

Page 50
Ceramic teppanyaki grills
陶板　*Toban*
LARGE:
Diameter: 13"　H: 3½"
SMALL:
Diameter: 9⅞"　H: 2"
Nagatani Ceramics/
Igamono Line

Page 51
Porridge pot

行平土鍋　*Yukihiranabe Donabe*
H: 5⅛" L with handle: 7⅞"
Pot only: 5½"
Takumi

Pages 52 & 53
Oden stew pot
おでん鍋　*Oden Nabe*
Capacity: 7 liters
With lid: H: 5½"　W: 11"
Aritsugu

Pages 54 & 55
Tempura pot
天ぷら鍋　*Tempura nabe*
Diameter: 10⅔"
H with handles: 5"
Aritsugu

Pages 56 & 57
Oyako pan　親子鍋　*Oyakonabe*
H with raised handle: 7⅞"
D: 6½"　H: 1"
Kiya

Omelet pan
卵焼鍋　*Tamagoyakinabe*
L with handle: 13"
L of pan: 6½"
W: 4¾"　H: 1⅛"
Kiya

Pages 60 & 61
Spatula　ヘラ　*Hera*
(beech)
SMALL: L: 11⅞" L: 14⅛"

Spatula
ヘラ　*Hera*
Chisha (persimmon wood)
LARGE: 15⅛"　MEDIUM: 12¼"
SMALL: 12"
Kiya

Pages 62 & 63
Aluminum ladle (shallow)
アルミお玉浅形
Arumi otama asagata
L: 11⅜"
Ladle diameter: 3⅓"
Aritsugu

Aluminum ladle (deep)
アルミお玉深形
Arumi otama fukagata
L: 11⅞" Ladle diameter: 3⅓"
Aritsugu

Brass Ladle
真ちゅう杓子　*Machyu Shakushi*
L: 19⅔" Ladle diameter: 3½"
Aritsugu

Wooden ladle
木製杓子　*Mokusei Shakushi*
LARGE:
L: 11⅞"　W: 4⅓"
Ladle diameter: 3⅓"
SMALL:
L: 10½"　W: 3½"
Ladle diameter: 3"

Pages 64 & 65
Stainless wire grill with 'legs'
or base
焼網足付　*Yakiami ashi-tsuki*
W: 8¼"　H: 2⅓"
Kiya

Stainless Wire grill, round
焼網（丸）*Yakiami (Maru)*
9½"
Kiya

Copper wire grill with base,
round
銅足付焼網丸
Do-ashi-tsuki Yakiami Maru
Aritsugu

Copper wire grill, with base,
square
銅足付焼網（角）
Do Ashitsuki Yakiami
Aritsugu

Copper wire grill with handles
for mochi rice cakes
もち焼網　*Mochi Yakiami*
Diameter: 7⅞"　H: ¾"
Aritsugu

Pages 66 & 67
Drop-lids　落し蓋　*Otoshibuta*
SMALL: 5½", H: 1"
LARGE: 8⅔", H: 1½"
Aritsugu

Page 68
Brush for sauces, for household use
タレ家庭用ばけ
Tare Kateiyoubake
MEDIUM:
L: 9¼"　Bristle length 1½"
Brush width 1½"
SMALL:
L: 9¼"　Bristle length: 1½"
Brush width: 1⅛"
Tora Fujimoto

For professional chefs
菓子刷毛胴巻職人用
Kashibake doummaki shokunin you
L: 10⅞"　Bristle length: 1½"

Brush width: 2"
Tora Fujimoto

Page 69
Cooking brushes of sheep's
wool
料理ハケ（白羊の毛）
Ryori bake (shirohitsuji)
L (all three): 9⅔"
LARGE: Bristle length: 1⅓"
Brush width: 2¼"
MEDIUM: Bristle length: 1⅓"
Brush width: 1½"
SMALL: Bristle length: 1⅓"
Brush width: 1⅛"
Aritsugu

Page 70
Cooking chopsticks
菜箸　*Saibashi*
L: 14½"
Kiya

Page 72
Colander for simmering foods
(bamboo)
しきざる／煮ざる（真竹）
Shikizaru or nizaru (madake)
H: 6⅔"　Diameter: 13"
Kiya

Page 73
Horse-hair Sieve (Hinoki body,
cherry tree bark ties)
馬毛うらごし　*Umakei Uragoshi*
Diameter: 8½"　H: 4"
Aritsugu

Page 76
Copper grater for garnishes
(Crane)
銅薬味 鶴形
Dou yakumi oroshi Tsuru
L: 4"　W: 3⅛"　H: ⅛"
Maker: Oyakoseisakujo
Kiya

Page 77
Copper grater for garnishes
(Turtle)
銅薬味 亀形
Dou yakumi oroshi Kame
L: 4⅛"　W: 2⅞"　H: ¼"
Maker: Oyakoseisakujo
Kiya

Page 78
Chinese Lotus Spoon (Slotted)
ちりれんげ　*Chirirenge*
8⅞"
Aritsugu

Page 79
Square Tofu Scoop
すくい角型 *Sukui Kadokata*
5³⁄₄"
Aritsugu

Round spoon (large)
丸型 (大) *Marukata (Dai)*
6⁷⁄₈"
Aritsugu

Spoon shape
スプーン形 *Spoon kata*
5²⁄₃"
Aritsugu

Chrysanthemum
菊形編 *Kikukataami*
8¹⁄₄"
Aritsugu

Round spoon (small)
丸形子 *Marugata (sho)*
6"
Aritsugu

Pages 82 & 83
Metal tipped chopsticks for
arranging food (Magnolia
Handle)
マナ箸 *Manabashi (Morizukebashi)*
10¹⁄₄"
Aritsugu

Bamboo chopsticks for arrang-
ing food
京風もりつけ箸
Kyo-fu Moritsukebashi
LARGE: 13" MEDIUM: 11"
SMALL 9"
Ichihara Heibei

Pages 84 & 85
Special Rice Servers
特上杓文子 *Tokujo Shamoji*
MEDIUM SIZE SAKURA CHERRY
WOOD: 8"
SMALL SEN MAGNOLIA WOOD: 7"
MEDIUM KEYAKI ZELKOVA: 8"
SMALL SAKURA CHERRY: 7¹⁄₂"
MEDIUM SEN MAGNOLIA WOOD: 8"
Kiya

Page 86
Rice Servers (Cypress)
杓子 *Shamoji*
EXTRA LARGE: 11²⁄₃"
LARGE: 9⁷⁄₈" MEDIUM: 8¹⁄₄"
SMALL: 7"
Temaki sushi you (for do-it-your-
self-sushi): 6"
Kiya

Pages 88 & 89
Sushi rice holder 飯台
Handai (also called *sushioke*)
W: 13" H: 3¹⁄₂"
5 cups of rice
Kiya

Page 90
Small *ohitsu* or rice holder with
shamoji
小びつ *Kobitsu*
W: 6²⁄₃" H: 5¹⁄₂" Shamoji: 6"
Kiya

Page 91
Mat for sushi rolls
まきす *Makisu*
10¹⁄₄" by 10¹⁄₄"
Aritsugu

Pages 92 & 93
Rice presses or molds
物相 *Mosou*
(Pine/matsu/松)
(Plum/ume/梅)
L: 6" D: 1³⁄₄"
Aritsugu

Pages 94 & 95
Rice ball press
おにぎり箱 *Onigiribako*
L: 11⁷⁄₈" D: 3¹⁄₈" H: 1³⁄₄"
Kiya

Page 95
Sushi press
押し寿司型 *Oshizushikata*
L: 7", H: 2¹⁄₂", D: 3¹⁄₂"
Kiya

Pages 98 & 99
Seiro and *sudare* cleaner
せいろ洗い *Seiro Arai*
Kame no ko

Teapot cleaner
きゅうす洗い *Kyusu Arai*
Fujimoto Tora

Sake Bottle cleaner
徳利洗い *Tokkuri Arai*
Fujimoto Tora

Fine pot cleaner
かるかや *Karukaya*
Kame no ko

For brushing counters clean of
flour and other powders
玉ホウキ *Tama Hoki Tosaka*
Takumi

All-purpose scrubber

たわし *Tawashi*
Kame no ko

Pages 100 & 101
Cleaning cloth
さらし布巾 *Sarashi Fukin*
22³⁄₄" x 22³⁄₄"
Seishichi Nakagawa Shoten

Page 102
Mini Tongs
ミニトング *Mini Tongu*
7"
Beniya Mingeiten

Bamboo Whisk
根竹 *Netake Madora*
6"
Beniya Mingeiten

Cherry whisk
チェリーマドラ *cheri madora*
6²⁄₃"
Beniya Mingeiten

Tofu prong 豆腐さし *Tofu Sashi*
7"
Kiya

Page 103
Knife Stones 砥石 *Toishi*

Grey
中 *Chu*
8" X 2²⁄₃" X 1¹⁄₈"

Red
平成 *Heisei*
8" X 2¹⁄₂" X 1¹⁄₃"

Beige
人造仕上げ *Jinzoshiage*
8¹⁄₄" X 3" X 1"
Aritsugu

Pages 104 & 105
Kappogi 割烹着
Various sizes available
Sold around Kappabashi

Geta 下駄
Various sizes available
Sold around Kappabashi

ACKNOWLEDGMENTS

I'd like to toast the craftspeople throughout Japan whose dedication and hard work have kept these tools alive. I am also very grateful to Ishida-san of Kiya and Koyama-san of Aritsugu who patiently answered my flurry of questions by phone and in person. (Many of the beautiful items in this book were graciously lent to us by these venerable companies.) The people at Benzai Mingeiten and Takumi were equally helpful. And without Ori Koyama, our stylist, we would have never got the job done. She helped with the selection, gathered all the items, and was a fount of information on matters throughout.

The tools were beautifully captured thanks to the wonderful work of photographer, Yasuo Konishi, my partner, and art director Kazuhiko Miki. Konishi's work is simple yet bold and so, too, Miki-san's design. It was very harmonious working with these men.

I must say "thank you" and *otsukaresama* to my wonderful editor, Greg Starr. And I should mention my parents, whose lives were ever enriched by living in Japan for two years in the late 1950s; by virtue, they instilled a love for me in this country and cuisine. Gesshinkyo, Waketokuyama and Koshiki: thank you for taking time to cooperate with us on this little culinary adventure. And I salute my friends and neighbors who reluctantly let me "expose" their charred and dented pots, rice paddles and cooking chopsticks. Finally, I'd like to express gratitude to all the wonderful chefs over the years who have manipulated these specialized tools in whipping up sumptuous delicacies for my benefit.

Kate Klippensteen
Tokyo, 2006

(英文版)クール・ツールズ
Cool Tools

2006年2月24日　第1刷発行

著　者　ケイト・クリッペンスティーン
写　真　小西康夫
発行者　富田 充
発行所　講談社インターナショナル株式会社
　　　　〒112-8652 東京都文京区音羽 1-17-14
　　　　電話 03-3944-6493 (編集部)
　　　　　　 03-3944-6492 (マーケティング部・業務部)
　　　　ホームページ　www.kodansha-intl.com
印刷・製本所　大日本印刷株式会社

落丁本・乱丁本は購入書店名を明記のうえ、講談社インターナショナル業務部宛にお送りください。送料小社負担にてお取替えします。なお、この本についてのお問い合わせは、編集部宛にお願いいたします。本書の無断複写(コピー)、転載は著作権法の例外を除き、禁じられています。

定価はカバーに表示してあります。